*THE MOST
    IMPORTANT
THING A MAN NEEDS
    TO KNOW ABOUT
THE REST OF HIS LIFE*

The Most Important Thing a Man Needs to Know About the Rest of His Life

TED W. ENGSTROM
Executive Director, World Vision

Fleming H. Revell Company
Old Tappan, New Jersey

Scripture quotations identified KJV are from the King James Version of the Bible.

Scripture quotations identified NAS are from the New American Standard Bible, Copyright © The LOCKMAN FOUNDATION 1960, 1962, 1963, 1968, 1971, 1972, 1973, 1975 and are used by permission.

Scripture quotations identified ASV are from the American Standard Version of the Revised Bible, copyrighted 1946 by the International Council of Religious Education, and are used by permission.

Scripture quotations identified AMPLIFIED are from AMPLIFIED BIBLE, OLD TESTAMENT, Copyright 1962, 1964 by Zondervan Publishing House, and are used by permission.

Scripture quotations identified LB are from The Living Bible, Copyright © 1971 by Tyndale House Publishers, Wheaton, Illinois 60187. All rights reserved.

Scripture quotations identified NEB are from The New English Bible. © The Delegates of the Oxford University Press and the Syndics of the Cambridge University Press 1961 and 1970. Reprinted by permission.

I AM LOVED © Copyright 1978 by William J. Gaither. International Copyright secured. All rights reserved. Used by permission of The New Benson Company, Inc., Nashville.

Reprint from MEN IN MID-LIFE CRISIS by Jim Conway © 1978 David C. Cook Publishing Co., Elgin, IL 60120. Used by permission.

Excerpts from *Aim's Guide to Financial Security* reprinted with permission from AIM, A Division of the American Association of Retired Persons. Copyright 1978.

Excerpts from RETIREMENT WITHOUT FEAR by Lee Butcher. Copyright © 1978. Reprinted by permission of Dow Jones & Company, Inc. All rights reserved.

Excerpts from PRIME TIME—MOVING INTO MIDDLE AGE WITH STYLE by Herb Barks. Copyright © 1978 by Thomas Nelson, Inc., Publishers. Reprinted by permission of Thomas Nelson, Inc., Publishers.

Excerpts from *The Middle-Age Crisis* by Barbara Fried. Harper & Row, New York, 1967. Used by permission.

"Easter's Story" by Dan Thrapp, Copyright, 1972, *Los Angeles Times.* Reprinted by permission.

Library of Congress Cataloging in Publication Data

Engstrom, Theodore Wilhelm, date
  The most important thing a man needs to know
about the rest of his life.

  1. Retirement—United States. 2. Middle age.
I. Title.
HQ1062.E54   646.7′9   81–1990
ISBN 0–8007–1254–4   AACR2

TO

Gordon Donald AND Jo Ann

Contents

Preface

This book is about *you*—you and your retirement years. I hope that you'll find it not only helpful, but warm and encouraging. It is, essentially, a "how to" book: "how to" prepare yourself in the years between age 35 and age 55 for those important, fruitful and significant retirement years to come.

You'll note as you read it that this book has a sense of urgency to it. That's because I seek constantly to encourage you in *early* preparation for the retirement years. This book suggests options aimed at a more active—and certainly a more involving —agenda during that significant time in your life.

Many books on "retirement" have been written for those planning to retire *soon.* This book, however, has been written for the person who wants to plan *now* for retirement some years later on.

* * *

I must express my deep appreciation for the immense help in this project given me by a dear friend, Gary Evans—a gifted researcher as well as an accomplished writer. Without his help and guidance, this book would never have been written. I am deeply indebted to Gary for his wonderful help.

TED W. ENGSTROM

Introduction

What you will be . . . you are now becoming.

The Most Important Thing a Man Needs to Know About the Rest of His Life is all about you . . . you, and the rest of your life! Which is a very good reason why you should read it!

This book was written to help you prepare for the most overlooked—yet potentially most fulfilling—period of your life: your retirement. (A period, by the way, that could include anywhere from one-fourth to one-third of your entire lifespan!)

No matter how limited your financial resources, your talents, or your abilities, I sincerely believe you can take the necessary steps now to insure a fulfilling and secure future. Your "second half" need *not* mean regret, disappointment, or want.

There is no doubt that the needed preparation for that second half will be easier if you're 35, more difficult if you're 55. But *it can be done* . . . provided you are willing to begin *now.*

But I also hope *The Most Important Thing a Man Needs to Know About the Rest of His Life* will help you prepare for something else: a future fresh with a new sense of promise and adventure as a child of God—and *that* future can begin right now!

What You Will Be . . . You Are Now Becoming

You will find that a strong current running through this book is the fact that avoiding an unhappy future depends directly upon what you do today. In fact, learning how to apply that truth *is* the first step in avoiding this possible problem.

Preparing for retirement means beginning to think differently about the future. That's why we'll be talking about how you see yourself: your worth as a person, your potential for growth, your feelings about growing older . . . even your feelings about death. Because what you think and how you feel

11

about these issues have much to do with how well you will be able to take hold of the future and make it work *for* you.

"But how can I begin to change the way I feel about these things?" you may ask.

If you are really serious about that question, there's more than hope—there's exciting challenge and a fulfilling future.

God Believes in New Things

Even a casual browsing of the Bible reveals that the Christian faith is all about "new things." The Bible says: "Therefore if any man is in Christ, he is a new creature; the old things passed away; behold, new things have come" (2 Corinthians 5:17 NAS). ". . . Behold, I make all things new . . ." (Revelation 21:5 KJV). "I will do a new thing . . ." (Isaiah 43:19 KJV).

This expresses much more than a conversion experience. It speaks of a life-style in which we recognize that His "mercies . . . . are new every morning" (Lamentations 3:22, 23 KJV). Changing the *now* so that our tomorrows can be brighter is exactly the "business" God is in! And, as we trust in His continuing work as our Savior, our failures and past sins are being redeemed. We can afford to look forward to tomorrow, then, for Jesus Christ brings fresh possibility and potential to each day. That means that whatever your age (or however you feel *about* your age), your future can be more fulfilling than your past.

Your fortieth birthday may have been the darkest day of your life. You might have said then, "It's all over—I might as well spend the rest of my days folding up my tent."

Well, I've got news for you. God wants to move you into a "new day," one that can bring a fulfilling future. He wants you to begin to walk in the land of the living—not the dying.

It's Okay to Plan for the Future

I've found that many Christians have serious questions about planning for the future. You, too, have probably heard people say, "I don't believe that God wants our minds to be so occupied with 'storing up for the future.' We shouldn't be so anxious about tomorrow: if we trust God, He'll take care of us."

Then you've probably heard the other side, too: "God gave

us minds, and He expects us to use them. He wants us to be responsible with what He has given us." This thought is often expressed in its extreme form in the familiar "God takes care of those who take care of themselves."

As with many such statements, there is a measure of practical, scriptural truth in that observation. However, a study of the Bible (together with some sanctified experience) reveals that there is seldom the need to choose between extremes. The truth usually lies somewhere in between.

Let's begin with the fact that if we trust Christ as Savior we have been spiritually born into a new family. Because we are now sons and daughters of God, we have birthrights—things we *own*. We have an inheritance.

Let's look at two of those important birthrights now.

We Can Be at Peace About the Future

First, we have the privilege of freedom from fear and anxiety about the future.

In the Sermon on the Mount, Jesus talks about the certainty of His provision for us. However, this message of comfort begins with some stern directives. In Matthew 6:19, Jesus tells us not to lay up treasure on earth, but rather in Heaven. He even takes it a step further by warning that material goods, which are intended to serve us, can become our masters. And "No one can serve two masters; for either he will hate the one and love the other, or he will hold to one and despise the other. You cannot serve God and mammon [riches]" (Matthew 6:24 NAS).

But why would a person ever serve riches, letting them become the all-important "object of his affections"? In the verses following, Jesus makes it clear that the reason for this unnatural servitude is anxiety—or fear about the future. Jesus depicts a person who, because of lack of faith in the Father's ability to provide, is actually serving riches, which he perceives to be his final security. He is filled with anxiety over "goods"; they have become his god.

In Matthew 6:25–34 the word *anxious* is used five times:

Do not be *anxious* for your life, as to what you shall eat
. . . (v. 25).

And which of you by being *anxious* can add a single cubit
to his life's span (v. 27)?

And why are you *anxious* about clothing (v. 28)?

Do not be *anxious* then saying, "What shall we eat? . . . (v.
31).

Therefore do not be *anxious* for tomorrow . . . (v. 34).

NAS, italics added.

Jesus is talking about an attitude of heart quite different
from that of responsible stewardship of what God has given.
Unremitting anxiety is a veritable worshipping at the shrine of
fear of the future. That is why Jesus says, "Seek first the Kingdom of God." Your king has become riches, because you are
afraid. *First,* let God rule in your heart.

The very word *anxiety* pertains to the future: it is fear over
what "might be." And such fear disallows trust in God.

The Apostle Paul has a remedy: "Be anxious for nothing, but
in everything by prayer and supplication with thanksgiving let
your requests be made known to God. And the peace of God,
which surpasses all comprehension, shall guard your hearts
and your minds in Christ Jesus" (Philippians 4:6,7 NAS).

Clearly, as Christians, we are not to be anxious about the
future. Once we put God's rule first in our hearts, our inheritance is peace of mind. "For God hath not given us the spirit
of fear; but of power, and of love, and of a sound mind" (2
Timothy 1:7 KJV).

God's power, love, and "soundmindedness" are the antidote
to our fear. And that soundmindedness ties into the second
birthright of the sons and daughters of God.

We Are Partners With God on Earth

Our second important birthright is the privilege of partnership with God on earth. And an important part of this partnership is sharing in the task of bringing God's provision into
being.

This partnership with God in accomplishing His purposes on
earth has historically been the source of much debate, because
it is rooted in the tension between the sovereignty of God and

the free will of man—the finite in partnership with the infinite. For our purposes, however, there is certainly no reason to become mired in a theological discussion. Rather, we can look at biblical examples of this partnership in action—examples that relate directly to the mind-set we need in preparing for our future.

God Gives That We May Possess

One thing was very clear to the people of Israel as they moved toward the Promised Land: God had given them that land. It was theirs. Hadn't the Lord told Moses on the plains of Moab across from Jericho, ". . . and you shall take possession of the land and live in it for I have given the land to you to possess it" (Numbers 33:53 NAS)?

Look closely, and you will find God's part of the partnership ("I have given the land to you") and man's ("to possess it"). And wherever we read of God's assuring Israel of their Promised Land, we usually find the partnership of God and man clearly expressed. Deuteronomy 2:24, for example: "Arise, set out. . . . Look! *I have given* Sihon the Amorite, king of Heshbon, and his land into your hand; *begin to take possession* and contend with him in battle" (NAS, italics added).

Perhaps the most inspiring example of this truth is the passage in 2 Chronicles where Jehoshaphat prays to God to save Judah from the attacking multitudes. In response to this supplication, God says: ". . . Do not fear or be dismayed because of this great multitude, for the battle is not yours but God's" (2 Chronicles 20:15 NAS).

There it is—our first birthright, stated very clearly—working in us, above us, and beneath us are the sovereign power and provision of God. We are therefore not to fear: it is not our battle. Yet, read on: "Tomorrow go down against them . . . . station yourselves, stand and see the salvation of the Lord on your behalf . . ." (vv. 16, 17).

Even though the battle was God's, the Lord required that they go out and face the enemy. It was their *task* to trod the ground and to claim it as theirs. (In this instance, God's people did not actually have to enter the fight. In most instances throughout the Old Testament, however, they did.) In faith, in planning, and even in the heat of battle they were in active partnership with God to possess the land.

In the New Testament, this partnership is more personal—and miraculous. As believers, we are the body of Christ. God's Spirit dwells within us, and He bids us to be His hands and His feet in bringing into visibility the Kingdom of God on earth. It is *His* power, *His* ability—and it is all to *His* glory. But at the same time, it is *our* hands, *our* feet, *our* minds. We must work with Him in establishing His kingdom, His rule, in the hearts and minds of all men and women on earth.

Mark 16 describes the ascension of the Lord, and then adds that the disciples "went out and preached everywhere, while the Lord *worked with them,* and confirmed the word . . ." (Mark 16:20 NAS, italics added).

In 1 Corinthians, chapters 2 and 3, the Apostle Paul refers to us as God's temple in whom His Spirit dwells. He even dares to say that we can have the mind of Christ. We are "God's fellow-workers" (1 Corinthians 3:9 NAS).

It is a miracle, and one that must be lived with in humility. God is and always will be the Lord of life, and we are but men and women who must continually seek His direction and who utterly depend upon the strength and grace He gives. But on the other hand we cannot deny the position of Sonship that He has given to us, and with it the very real responsibility to work with Him, using our ability, time, and resources to accomplish His purposes.

In summary, God has provided for our future, and it is our birthright to be at peace about that. But part of the miracle of being born into the family of God is that He has chosen us to actualize that which He has provided. "Have I not commanded you? Be strong and courageous! Do not tremble or be dismayed, for the Lord your God is with you wherever you go" (Joshua 1:9 NAS).

Joshua commanded the officers of the people, saying: "Pass through the midst of the camp and command the people, saying, *'Prepare provisions for yourselves,* for within three days you are to cross Jordan, to go in to *possess the land* which the Lord your God *is giving you, to possess it'* " (Joshua 1:11 NAS, italics added).

* * *

"A man's mind plans his way, but the Lord directs his steps and makes them sure" (Proverbs 16:9 AMPLIFIED).

All of God's promises for a fulfilling future are ours; He has given us every good thing. But it is our responsibility to "take the land," using obedient faith expressed in positive action. Let's move forward together, confidently, into that future!

1
Welcome to the Better Half!

At twenty years of age the will reigns; at thirty the wit; at forty the judgment.

BENJAMIN FRANKLIN

You really couldn't be more fortunate: you're moving into the rewarding and productive half of your life . . . the half that can include a fulfilling, active retirement.

During the first half of life, you explored life's parameters. You questioned, ventured, sought . . . even dared. You reached out to touch both the possibilities and the liabilities of living. In doing so, you no doubt experienced both the "thrill of victory" and the "agony of defeat." But you learned—and you grew.

Life's second half will allow you to do all of the above—and more. It has room for just as much challenge and adventure, but with an important difference.

You are now viewing your future from a different perspective, one that allows you to use the wisdom and judgment that your experience has bought (and paid for). And that's a big bonus!

But there's another reason why you're fortunate: America is finally waking up to just how important *you* are!

We Have a Revolution on Our Hands!

Whether you are 35 or 45 or 55, you are part of a social revolution that is bringing drastic social, economic, and political changes to our country. They're calling it the "Retirement Revolution."

America is beginning to recognize both the needs and the untapped potential of the millions of men and women in—or moving into—retirement. Of course, the critical question is, will you be ready to take advantage of the opportunities this new awareness can mean for you? Or will you miss out, because you failed to prepare?

Most people don't begin to make serious plans for retirement until they're on the verge of leaving work. When actually, the time to start preparing is when you're in your 30s and 40s.

The reasons are numerous—and a bit frightening. (More about that later in the book.) For the purposes of this chapter, however, be assured that preparing for the second half of life is important if for no other reason than understanding the "Retirement Revolution"—from which *you* can personally benefit.

Retirement Is a New Idea

Our concept of retirement is changing. Retirement no longer means simply the termination of one's working years. Increasingly, it is a dynamic transition to a widening, more wholesome pattern of challenges and opportunities. Retirement is also no longer a luxury enjoyed by a few—nor is it merely a period of inactivity for the "too-old-to-work-but-too-young-to-die" set.

The idea of retirement, as a matter of fact, is a relatively recent phenomenon. As recently as the turn of the century, few people lived to spend any appreciable time in retirement. Those who did manage to grow old simply kept on working until they died.

You might say that retirement came of age (that age being 65!) with the advent of Social Security in the 1930s. The decision to base retirement on a certain age, and apply it to the general working force, was made by a small group of New Deal experts who had been given the task of drafting the Social Security Act of 1935.

The decision was made at a time of unprecedented unemployment, with an estimated 25 percent of the labor force unemployed. Consequently, one aim of the legislation was to remove older people from the labor force, while at the same time providing them with retirement benefits.

Today, however, experts in the field of aging—to say nothing of many retirees themselves—understand that prolonged periods of enforced inactivity are physically, mentally, and emotionally unhealthy. Mandatory retirement is increasingly seen as discriminatory, limiting, as it does, individual freedom and imposing undue hardship on persons who wish to and/or need to keep working.

Because of the Social Security Act, two generations of Americans have been raised on the notion of "65 and out" (an experience sometimes sweetened by a gold watch and a pension). However, because of the effects of the Retirement Revolution, many people moving into retirement today (and tomorrow) will find that getting a new job—or hanging onto the present one—may be easier than at any time in the last 50 years.

But what forces have brought about this social revolution?

More People Can Afford to Retire

Today in the United States, among people 65 and over, only one man in five and one woman in 12 are in the work force. One clear reason for this is that more and more Americans are financially able to retire. Social Security benefits have been expanded, for one thing. For another, full pensions are paid at age 65 (although some prefer to retire at an earlier age with reduced benefits). Nearly half of all workers in the private economy are covered by pension plans, many with retirement provisions at ages 60, 55, and even 50!

Stan Jameson was a successful public accountant in Canada for 28 years. At the young age of 53, he "retired" from his business, entered theological seminary, and earned his master's degree in religion. He's now putting his years of accounting experience to work as the business manager of a church. According to Stan: "People have always had a lot of life left at 50 and 55, but nowadays many more people can make enough to be able to retire. They can make a unique contribution in retirement because they don't have to worry about making a living. Therefore, they can make some tougher choices, take some greater risks, and serve in areas that can't offer a living wage."

Supporting this fact of retiree affluence, John Meeker, president of Del E. Webb Development Company, estimates that most residents of Sun City, Arizona, have annual incomes between $10,000 and $20,000. About 70 percent of the buyers into this well-known retirement community pay cash for their homes, using money derived from the sales of their previous dwellings.[1]

Motor-home dealers say that retired people are among their best customers. Models with kitchens, dining areas, and sleeping quarters, priced at an average of $27,000, are within easy reach of many retirees.

But there are still other factors that are firing this revolution. Dramatic social and demographic changes are affecting the *number* of people in retirement: the age of retirement, the length of the retirement period, and the shifting proportion of older persons remaining active in the work force.

You'll Probably Live Longer Than Your Granddad

It was not until this century that a majority of Americans began to live to enjoy even their middle years. As recently as 1900, life expectancy in the United States was about age 48 for a man and 51 for a woman. Only 10 percent of the population was "middle-aged."

Even as recently as 1920, the average life expectancy of American men was fewer than 54 years. Now, the average is 72 for men and nearly 78 for women. People reaching 65 this year can expect to live, on average, almost 15 more years.

This trend will probably continue. By the year 2050, it is projected that life expectancy will have increased another three years for men and another four years for women.

According to *50 Plus Magazine,* 3,700 Americans retire every day. And, adds this retirement journal, insurance statistics show that these new retirees have longer to live than many of them suppose. A man who is 65, for example, can expect to live until 81; a woman of the same age can expect to live until she is nearly 85.[2]

Fortunately, this increased longevity does not mean that the last twenty years or so of life must be endured with impaired health and physical mobility. On the contrary, many of today's 70-year-olds resemble their 50-year-old counterparts at the beginning of the century. Much of this is due to advances and improvements in nutrition, health care, and environmental sanitation. Quite a different picture from Whistler's mother, who epitomizes old age—and was only 44 when she sat for the famous painting!

What does this longevity mean to you? It means simply that by the time you retire you may be able to look forward to twenty more years of active living—half as many more years as an entire life span just a few short generations ago!

However, more people, living longer, are bound to have dramatic repercussions on our nation as a whole. That's exactly what's happening—and it's where we begin to see the real impact of the Retirement Revolution.

America Is Maturing

We are in the midst of a population transformation—a change from a younger to an older society. In the past 100 years, the population of the United States has increased by a factor of five, while the number of those over 65 has increased by a factor of 16!

In addition to increased longevity, there is another reason for this population transformation. Joseph Califano, former Secretary of the Department of Health, Education, and Welfare, says that "The baby boom following World War II will become a 'senior boom' in the early 21st century. In 1940, 7 percent of the population was 65 and over; today [1978] it is 11 percent; by 2030 it will be nearly 20 percent."[3]

We used to hear much about the "greening of America." Now more and more frequently we hear about the "graying of America." This is reflected in magazine and television advertising, for example. In our consumer-oriented society, people of middle age to retirement age are being increasingly catered to as an increasingly profitable market for goods and services. In spite of the prospect of continuing inflation and a volatile economy, the highly respected Kiplinger organization recently gave this reason for the predicted growing economy in the 1980s:

> A new surge in consumer demand is building for the '80s . . . sparked partly by shifts in population mix . . . the spendingest age groups. Within the next 10 years, there will be 11 million more 25- to 40-year-olds, totally of 60 million . . . the baby boom of people of '50s and '60s coming of age . . . .[4]

They added that the '80s would bring "20 percent more people age 65 and over . . . an older country."

All about us we see signs of this new awareness of longevity. Concessions are being made to senior citizens in many areas of business—especially to the more elderly and the financially disabled. Pharmacies offer discounts on prescriptions and vitamins. Theaters reduce prices on certain days. Public transportation must offer half fares to senior citizens in order to qualify for federal aid.

It is a belated awareness, true, but make no mistake—it has come.

The Coming of Gray Power

The political implications of this trend are enormous. Until the last decade politicians paid little attention to older Americans because their numbers were fewer and they were disorganized and splintered. Now there are numerous organizations speaking and agitating on behalf of a healthier, better-educated retiree population, and they are making their voices heard—loudly. Groups such as the Gray Panthers, the American Association of Retired Persons, Retired Teachers of America and many others are pushing for "senior power," and they are getting it.[5]

One of the more obvious effects of political "gray power" was the change of the mandatory retirement age from 65 to 70.

At present, a little more than 10 percent of the population in the United States is 65 or over. Yet this group represents 20 percent of the adult population, and an even larger percentage of the voting population. In addition, the same age group has a number of militant and other special interest groups who successfully championed raising the mandatory retirement age in businesses and industry. The resulting demographic and political configuration was overwhelming. As one politician put it, "voting against the extension of mandatory retirement was like voting against motherhood and the flag."[6]

(Incidentally, some Washington experts on aging say it is almost a foregone conclusion that Congress will pass a law by the early 1980s that will completely wipe out forced retirement.)

It remains to be seen how this trend will affect retirement patterns across the country. Some sociologists predict significant changes in work patterns, for example. Each succeeding generation of older people is more active and better educated. Economic and continued demographic changes will quite likely increase work opportunities for older people. The needs and desires of a whole new living generation will no doubt produce new demands and jobs.

As is the case during any time of change, there are crosscurrents of opinion and trends. One such countertrend is toward early retirement. Many are choosing to retire early, either into second careers or into lives of leisure, travel, or perhaps volunteer activity. And this is happening along with the crusade for greater freedom to stay working at one's career.

A retirement expert on the National Industrial Conference Board, a prominent business research organization, has said, "People want to retire while they are still young and healthy enough to enjoy the activities of their choice."[7] Research suggests, however, that dissatisfied workers (and those with better pension plans) seem to be more likely to retire earlier.

> The experience of Sears-Roebuck, Polaroid, and several insurance companies which have already introduced flexible retirement, shows that at least 50% of those workers reaching age 65 remain on the job. . . .[8]

Many gerontologists also oppose the early-retirement trend. They cite the greater political activity of older Americans, and point to the results of surveys of retirees over 65, many of whom claimed they would still be working if they had not been forced out of their jobs.

You Can Enjoy Creative Retirement

The encouraging thing that this discussion reveals is that many of today's retirees have the benefit of a *creative choice*

—to work or not to work. Whether to stay in their careers longer, or to begin new part-time careers that allow more time for leisure or helping others is up to them.

This is the real "plus" of the revolution—the creative opportunity for growth, fulfillment, and ministry in retirement.

Enjoying the Freedom of Choice

Bud and Joan Jenkins have always been blessed with "green thumbs." They were challenged, after retirement, with the prospect of growing orchids at home. Their success in orchid production soon reached a semicommercial level, and today they have a not-too-demanding business that is both enjoyable and income-producing.

Harman Gardner is part of a nomadic crew of retirees that rolls into towns in their recreational vehicles, bearing hammers, saws, wrenches, paintbrushes—and a mission to fix up struggling churches and chapels. Says Gardner: "I took a year enjoying life after I retired, traveled around, then asked the Lord what I could do for Him and my fellow man and still enjoy retirement years. . . . We usually work three days a week, play three days and pray on the seventh. We're out to double our lives after retirement and have fun doing it."[9]

Lucille and Clifton Garrard were a little late in getting started, but a few years ago they sat down to decide what they were going to do after retirement. Today they are the designers and manufacturers of Heirloom Dolls—original bisque dolls that are not only beautifully made but unusual enough to delight doll collectors of any age. (The price range for the dolls begins at $200.)[10]

Dr. F. J. Thompson recently retired after 30 years as a teacher and administrator in schools and colleges in Minnesota, Oregon, and California. He plans to write at least two books (already outlined), dealing with problems of governing of schools, as well as a more personal one on Thompson family history.[11]

Frona Tuetten dreamed of being a missionary since she was nine years old. After her husband died in 1974, she asked God, "What do you want me to do with my life now, Lord?" Her question was answered when she saw an application form for volunteer workers in a mission's paper. A few short months later she found herself working in an Austrian chalet used as a mission center for European evangelism. Her task? Superintendent of housework—and she loves every minute of it.[12]

Charles Honn, a retired school superintendent from Pleasant Valley, California, says retirement has given him an opportunity to spend more time with one of his favorite hobbies— woodworking. He enjoys doing "cabinet-type work" and furniture rebuilding, and creating wood carvings. He is currently using his carpentry talents to help his son remodel his home in Los Angeles.[13]

To a 73-year-old retired physician in Nebraska, retirement means "a chance to do the medical snooping that I never had a chance to do when I had my practice. I think I'm getting more satisfaction now than at any time in my 43 years in practice. I'm doing nutritional research among the very young and very old, poor blacks and whites."

A retired bank examiner, long active in his church, accepted its request to "look over the books" and see whether they could be put in better order. What he found convinced him that the church needed a nearly full-time financial officer. (He took the job, without pay.)

These are people of a new era—an era in which the retiree can enjoy the freedom of choice. With a little planning and forethought, creative retirement is entirely possible—and it's not only an exciting prospect for you, but a boon for our country as well.

> The aging folk are taking over. Thirty-five to forty million of us emerging to save America from its follies. We are led not by wrinkled rheumy-eyed patriarchs with cracked voices, but mostly by middle-aged gents and gals who still have an abundance of energy. They are modern Decision Makers, leading us in a second American Revolution.[14]

You are a part of this great possibility. You have (I hope) your health, your God-given ability to dream, and—fortunately— *time.* Time in which to plan, pray, and believe for God's very best.

All this and heaven too? Well . . . why not?

As I said . . . welcome to the second half!

*   *   *

I will be your God through all your lifetime, yes, even when your hair is white with age. I made you and I will care for you. I will carry you along and be your Savior.

Isaiah 46:4 LB

But the good man walks along in the ever-brightening light of God's favor; the dawn gives way to morning splendor.
. . .

Proverbs 4:18 LB

But my God shall supply all your need according to his riches in glory by Christ Jesus.

Philippians 4:19 KJV

Source Notes

1. "Choosing a Lifestyle—A Look at Five Ways," *U. S. News & World Report,* February 26, 1979, p. 60.
2. "Longevity Imperils Early Retirement," *The Idaho Statesman,* July 24, 1978.
3. *A Special Kiplinger Report: The 1980's—A Fresh Look* (Washington, D.C.: The Kiplinger Washington Editors, Inc., 1979), p. 1.
4. Ibid.
5. Lee Butcher, *Retirement Without Fear* (Princeton, N.J.: Dow Jones Books, 1978), p. 137.
6. Henry M. Wallfesh, *The Effects of Extending the Mandatory Retirement Age* (New York: AMACOM, 1978), p. 9.
7. Jerry Flint, "Early Retirement Is Growing in U.S.," *The New York Times,* July 10, 1977.
8. Jeffrey Sonnenfeld, "Dealing With the Aging Work Force," *Harvard Business Review,* November-December 1978, p. 82.
9. Russell Chandler, "Nomadic Crew Helps Churches in Need," *Los Angeles Times,* March 12, 1980, Part 1A, p. 5.
10. Winnie McFarland, "Retired Teacher Finds New Career," *Whittier* (Calif.) *Daily News,* February 20, 1980.
11. *South Pasadena* (Calif.) *Review,* January 30, 1980, p. 1.
12. Jean Marie Christie, "Soap Suds and Border Crossings," *Eternity,* March 1980, p. 56.
13. Linda Williams, "Preparation Key to Enjoyable Retire-

ment," *Oxnard* (Calif.) *Press Courier,* February 17, 1980, p. 9.

14. Oren Arnold, *The Second Half of Your Life* (Irvine, Calif.: Harvest House Pubs. Inc., 1979), p. 16.

2
... And Now the Bad News

There was a wise man in the East whose constant prayer was that he might see today with the eyes of the future.

ALFRED MERCIER

You've heard the good news: your second half can be the better half—and your retirement can be the most productive period of your life.

Now for the bad news: retirement can be a bitter disappointment. It can seem longer than a lifetime. For thousands, it is hell on earth.

And to qualify, all you have to do is . . . *nothing.*

Yes, sad to say, the underside of the retirement coin reveals tens of thousands of people who looked upon retirement as something life "owes" them.

Retirement is seen as the quiet harbor at the end of life's voyage. To reach the harbor, you just point your ship toward "old age" and set the instruments on "automatic pilot." Then you wait until age 65 or 70, and one morning you wake up and find yourself at "retirement harbor."

The sad truth, though, is that the majority never make the harbor. The "automatic pilot" just can't navigate around the unseen shoals and reefs that guard the approach. As a result, thousands live out their lives broken and shattered, with only a distant, tantalizing view of their lifelong retirement goal.

There just *is* no effortless, automatic course toward retirement. Retirement represents one of life's major transitions—and a transition can bring great fulfillment . . . or great tragedy.

Retirement Can Mean "You Lose"

Research indicates that the personal losses involved in the role transition from that of worker to that of retired person involve not only the loss of settings in which skills are performed and challenges are met, but also concomitant financial changes. A variety of other losses which may have equal or even greater consequences for the individual includes: loss of a principal source of social contact; loss of opportunities for problem solving; loss of mastery of resources available for problem solving; and loss of a major reference group.[1]

It's quite easy for us to take our vocations for granted. But for a man especially, "the job" means far more than a paycheck. Just think of what work does for us:

First, our work gives us a *sense of place.* We know who we are and where we fit. Isn't one of the first questions people ask when they meet you, "What do you do for a living?"

Second, our work gives us *leverage in the world.* Our organization or trade stands behind us in terms of things like credit ratings, social support, and life insurance and other fringe benefits.

Third, our daily work gives us a *goal orientation.* At work, we share a common task with others, a task in which we have a common responsibility and for which we feel a common drive. This gives us something to look forward to, as well as a feeling of accomplishment.

Fourth, our place, our ability, or our position gives us *prestige*—not only with our neighbors, but with ourselves. It's satisfying to know that this building, this product, this project, or these people are what they are because of what we have been able to do.

Fifth, our career gives us an *opportunity to help others* in the community, and to feel responsible—to feel that we are needed.

Now, what happens when these elements of meaning and security are suddenly taken from us? We feel as if we are floating in a vacuum. Our mobility is reduced. Our sense of direction is gone. Our sense of self-worth can be destroyed.

Sigmund Freud wrote in *Civilization and Its Discontents:* "Stressing the importance of work has a greater effect than any other technique of living in binding the individual more closely to reality; in his work he is at least securely attached to a part of reality, the human community."[2]

Dr. Marvin Sussman, director of the Institute of the Family

and the Bureaucratic Society at Case Western Reserve University, says people often regard retirement as a "demotion," and as a result they are faced with adjusting to both a sharp reduction in income and an entirely new life role. "This can lead to 'withdrawal symptoms' as severe as those usually associated with long-term illness."[3]

The American Medical Association says, "Considerable medical evidence is available to indicate that the sudden cessation of productive work and earning power of an individual, caused by compulsory retirement at the chronological age of sixty-five, often leads to physical and emotional deterioration and premature death."[4]

Dean Henley was just such a man who failed to plan for the changes of retirement. His goal was the top echelon of management in a computer sales company; all his activities and studies were focused on that single purpose. He surrounded himself with friends in the same business, and whenever they were together they "talked shop." He loved his family but—when it came to allotting time and attention—the job came first.

When he retired, his major interest in life—his "life-support" system, if you will—was severed. There was nothing for him to do. He had not cultivated other activities, and—even more tragic—he had no sustaining spiritual faith that could help bring positive change to his shattered view of himself and his world. His sense of self had been taken away, and he was bankrupt.

For the unprepared person, then, retirement—especially compulsory retirement—can amount to telling a person who has lived a productive life, "You are no longer of value."

Retirement Can Bring You Time—and Trouble

In addition, the unprepared person is usually forced to deal with such feelings of loss in the context of a tremendous "time gap": retirement can mean more than 2,000 new "free" hours a year.

Perhaps "free" time is the wrong description. For some it can be a terrible weight. This is particularly so among people who make the mistake of concentrating their retirement plans on one glorious fling—a cruise, for instance. They bask in four or five weeks of pleasure, and then return home to a void and a glut of time.

Idle time can be a poisonous commodity in a relationship. Couples may find the new constant closeness very difficult to accept. Wives strain for patience; but who is so saintly as to bear with equanimity the helpful comments of a husband who has nothing else to do but hang around home fretting because the hall table hasn't been dusted or a bed hasn't been made.[5]

Dr. Virginia L. Boyack describes all too many retired people when she says: "The person is retired from work; his or her income usually drops by about half, and the pattern of familial or other social relationships may be altered. During this time, over one-half of the women are widowed, and about one-fourth of the men become widowers. Most people have mixed emotions about this event called 'retirement.' There is a sense of relief felt by many of the prospect of release from work-a-day drudgery, but also apprehension about financial security. . . ."[6]

Those last two words touch a major "sore spot" of unprepared retirement: financial security—or perhaps we should say, financial *in*security.

Retirement Can Be the Road to Near-Poverty

It is a paradox of our society that though we are entering a period in which there are more opportunities than ever before for a fulfilling retirement—and in which, furthermore, more people are earning enough to make a secure retirement possible—retired people still comprise the fastest growing poverty group in the United States!

By far, more older persons are living in poverty than any other age group in America today; 15.3 percent of our senior citizens, or 3.3 million elderly people, were living in poverty in 1975. . . . In recent years, with older persons becoming more and more numerous and growing into a strong political force in this country, government programs and benefits for the aged have increased substantially. But

because of dramatic increases in the cost of living, much of
the income gains older people have made in recent years
have been whittled away by inflation.[7]

Why this problem among this particular age-group? One
very significant reason is given by Dr. Robert N. Butler, director of the National Institute of Aging. He points out that many
of the retired poor *became poor only after they retired.* True,
Social Security has increased greatly since it first came into
being and paid its first benefit—an average of a princely $22.50
a month in 1940. But it remains today what it was designed to
be: "The floor upon which a person can build his or her retirement protection. Because of inflation, sometimes it can become more like the basement."[8]

Financial planners vary on their advice as to just how much
income is needed after retirement. Some say 60 percent of a
person's pre-retirement income is necessary—others, as much
as 80 percent.

> There is very little room for belt tightening in retiring.
> People's desires don't change simply because they have
> stopped working. . . . Regarding the fact that many advisors
> say that you won't be buying many of the things in retire-
> ment that you now need working full time, the middle class
> retiree will want to take up or do other things they don't
> have time to do now, like golf, photography, entertaining,
> or travel.[9]

Another serious consideration is that even though one
might look toward the income available from a part-time job
during retirement, people can overestimate their physical ca-
pacities, or they may face unexpected medical problems. In
addition, job-related expenses often gnaw away at the extra
income.

> Women especially need to give close attention to providing
> for income in their old age. On the average, they live
> longer than men and therefore need income longer. They
> are less likely than men to qualify for pensions, and their
> Social Security benefits are likely to be meager because of
> lower earnings and fewer working years.[10]

In a study conducted by the Institute for Interdisciplinary Studies in Minneapolis, some 194,000 Americans over 65 responded to questionnaires. The following is a brief profile of these retirees:

> Most lived alone or with a spouse, but a "disproportionate" number lived in either retirement or nursing homes. About half owned their homes, and were responsible for their maintenance.
>
> Just over half of the retirees said they had difficulty making ends meet. More than a third had a hard time even paying for housing. Almost two-thirds said they had no money for the "little extras."
>
> Eighteen percent were still working part-time. Half of those who were working said they did so solely for financial reasons.
>
> Twenty-five percent said they had an illness they couldn't afford to have treated.
>
> Almost a third had difficulty getting around because they had no car, were unable to drive, or were too far from public transportation.
>
> Most said they needed help in preparing wills or other legal documents.
>
> Seventy-eight percent said they were happy and liked the neighborhoods where they lived. However, 22 percent felt unwanted, and 17 percent of these said they had nothing to live for.[11]

The Silent Partner of Financial Insecurity

You might feel that this is enough bad news about what can happen if you drift toward retirement on "automatic pilot." But I would be less than fair if I didn't warn you about still another facet of financial insecurity.

Some have called it the "villain of the 1970s"; however, it was a villain with no more than a "popgun" in comparison to what we face in the '80s. I'm talking about The New and Improved Inflation.

Listen to this quote from Lee Butcher's excellent book *Retirement Without Fear,* published in 1978:

> . . . There is every reason to believe that the cost of living will keep rising on the order of 6 percent a year . . . That 6 percent rate, year after year, means that the dollar of today will buy only a little over 50 cents worth of goods and services ten years from now. And unless your nest egg keeps getting more padding as the years go by, your retirement plans will surely go awry.[12]

Good advice. But consider this: as *this* book is being written —a short two years after Butcher's—the inflation rate has risen to 18 percent a year! Further, *U.S. News & World Report* says that if the present 18 percent annual rate of inflation continues, consumer prices will double by April, 1984—a mere four years from the time this book is being written.[13]

Sound unbelievable? If you read your newspaper—and understand something about the foment and volatility of our current economic scene—it is all too believable.

U.S. News and World Report tries to end its report on a more optimistic note:

> Administration economic advisors hold out hope that by year-end prices will be advancing at an annual rate of less than 10 percent. But many private business forecasters are less optimistic.[14]

A hearing of the congressional Special Committee on Aging gave this summary of the effects of inflation on the retired:

> It is widely assumed that the elderly suffer severely from the effects of inflation, because their income tends to be fixed and their assets, denominated in inflation dollars, tend to decline in value. On the whole the elderly have not been successful in protecting their dollar assets by hedging investment techniques. Owning a home remains one of the best means of hedging against inflation. Small amounts of savings deposited with institutions or invested in Government savings bonds return no real interest at recent levels of persistent inflation. . . . Indeed, at present levels of infla-

tion, small savings accounts actually lose money for the elderly in terms of purchasing power. As the savings erode away during longer periods of elevated rates of inflation, the elderly become increasingly dependent upon the government, losing their independence and dignity in the process.[15]

Let me tell you something about the statement you've just read. That very saddening picture of the plight of tens of thousands of retired people was drawn when the rate of inflation was 7 percent. You might want to read it again, realizing that the inflation rate has more than doubled!

Listen to the impassioned warning from a 75-year-old former top executive with 35 years of service for two of America's most respected organizations: "Find a way to warn young people against basing retirement plans on conditions as they are when the plan is initiated."

When You Plan, Expect the Unexpected

This was something that Douglas Murray, a 70-year-old former building contractor, didn't understand. His current income of $600 a month signifies a severely restricted retirement. Because inflation has reduced his dollar purchasing power by half, retirement has come to mean "a chance to regret my own stupidity. I knew very well the effects of inflation. I would complain about it every day when I had to figure material and labor on a job and try to eke out a profit. But I never connected it with retirement dollars. I never considered that my retirement dollars wouldn't buy any more than my construction dollars."

Florence McIntire's husband had earned over $50,000 a year as an executive for a pharmaceutical company. When the doctors discovered he had cancer he was forced to retire. He had always believed in moving up the income ladder, and had changed companies whenever he saw a better opportunity. However, as a result, he had never stayed in one place long enough to earn a pension or qualify for a good medical insurance plan, and he had never invested in anything but those consumer goods that would reflect his current affluent position.

Florence's husband's cancer operation and long convalescence used up most of their $50,000 in savings. When her husband died, remaining medical bills forced her to file for bankruptcy. Creditors eventually foreclosed on her home, and —for the rest of her days—she had to live literally hand to mouth, at the "mercy" of public welfare.

In his book *The Retirement Threat,* Tony Lamb recounts the story of a 69-year-old former oil company geologist, retired since 1973. The geologist and his wife thought they "had it made" when they paid off the mortgage of their handsome, tile-roofed stucco home in Alamo, Texas. But that was before inflation caught up with them. In 1973, their home was assessed for tax purposes at $55,980, which obligated the geologist to pay property taxes of $1,830. By 1975, inflation had pushed the assessed value to $122,000, boosting their property taxes to $3,791!

The geologist's words speak for themselves: "I just can't afford to pay my taxes. I'm sick about it. I'll have to get some work somewhere or give up everything. That's not easy at my age. Twice now I've been put out of jobs on mandatory age restrictions. I just hope I can find something at around $2.50 an hour. My wife and I are at our wits' end. Neither of us has had a solid night's sleep in four months."[16]

Enough bad news, you say. What about hope . . . or *is* there any hope? The answer is yes—lots of hope! But it takes planning. And, for some reason, most people—even those who see retirement looming dead ahead—resist thinking about and planning for the future.

Experts in the field of retirement planning say that many people deliberately avoid thinking about the future—even though gerontologist Woodrow Hunter of the University of Michigan says, "The time to start preparing for retirement is when you're in your 30s and 40s."[17]

A 1977 article in *The Wall Street Journal* quoted three bank officials who specialize in financial counseling. One said that fewer than 25 percent of the executives he deals with have systematic savings plans. Another stated that in 20 percent of the interviews he conducted, either the husband or wife lacked a prepared will. A third counselor said that "even among the 50-year-old executives, fewer than one-third have had any real idea of how they will finance their retirement."[18]

And these executives probably dealt with *corporate* financial planning every day!

Henry J. Moore, vice-president for Financial Planning at the brokerage firm of Merrill Lynch, says: "The biggest mistake people make is to start financial planning only three to five years before retirement, and by that time a lot of things are set in concrete."[19]

A 1979 study by Louis Harris and Associates indicates that: "Forty-eight percent of employees between 50 and 65 years of age (and 58% among all employees) have not given any thought to how much money they will need when they finally retire."[20]

In another study, Harris and Associates reported that "most older people regretted not having planned better. Such regrets were primarily focused on financial concerns." In addition:

> 26% of those surveyed mentioned that if they had known what things would be like today, they would have tried to save more, acquired more insurance, or invested more in property, land or some other type of investment.

> In addition, 14% of the older respondents would have completed more education, while 9% would have planned their careers differently in order to guarantee themselves greater security in their old age.

> Additional data indicated that 76% missed the money the job produced . . . 73% missed the people at work . . . 62% missed work itself . . . and 59% missed the feeling of being useful.[21]

Poverty of Spirit—the Worst Kind

Many of the regrets and disappointments above, as revealing as they may seem, hide an even deeper despair—a despair that comes from an inner emptiness, an inner wasteland, all too common among the retired.

If a person has an abiding faith in God, however, even financial hardship can be borne. If, through faith in Christ, he has the assurance of eternal life, if he knows he is as much a part of eternity as of time, then even the pain of loneliness, illness, or broken relationships can be endured.

But if there is no hope, no faith, nothing to live for beyond this life, that person knows only the worst kind of poverty—a poverty of spirit.

Father Congreve said, "It is not years that make souls grow old, but having nothing to love, nothing to hope for."[22]

That need not be the testimony of anyone reading this book. The Bible says, "The godly shall flourish . . . . Even in old age they will still produce fruit and be vital and green" (Psalms 92:12, 14 LB).

It is important for each one of us to understand the tragic implications of an unplanned future—implications that can be social, financial, emotional, spiritual, or "all of the above." But the "good news" is that you have the opportunity to choose differently. You *can* choose to plan for a meaningful future.

Psalms 25:12 says, "Where is the man who fears the Lord? God will teach him how to choose the best."

"The best" is letting God change your perspective on the future.

"The best" is joining with Him in planning His best for you.

Source Notes

1. Virginia L. Boyack, "Preparing for Retirement: Crisis or Challenge?" Hearing Before the Sub-committee on Retirement Income and Employment of the Select Committee on Aging, House of Representatives, Ninety-fifth Congress, Second Session (Washington, D.C.: U. S. Government Printing Office, 1978), p. 58.
2. Sigmund Freud, *Civilization and Its Discontents* (Honolulu: Hogarth Press, 1930), p. 34.
3. Lee Butcher, *Retirement Without Fear* (Princeton, N.J.: Dow Jones Books, 1978), p. 83.
4. Ibid., p. 68.
5. "Creative Retirement," *The Royal Bank of Canada Monthly Newsletter,* September 1978, p. 2.
6. Boyack, op. cit., p. 59.
7. Rudolph T. Danstedt, Hearing Before the Special Committee on Aging, United States Senate, Ninety-fifth Congress, Second

Session (Washington, D.C.: U. S. Government Printing Office, 1978), p. 280.

8. Edmund LeBreton, *Plan Your Retirement Now So You Won't Be Sorry Later* (Washington, D.C.: U. S. News & World Report Publishers, 1974), p. 106.

9. Tony Lamb and Dave Duffy, *The Retirement Threat* (Los Angeles: J. P. Tarcher, Inc., 1977), pp. 12, 23.

10. "It's Never Too Early to Plan," *U. S. News & World Report,* February 26, 1979, p. 56.

11. Butcher, op. cit., p. 3, 4.

12. Butcher, op. cit., p. 7.

13. "How to Survive Inflation," *U. S. News & World Report,* April 7, 1980, p. 25.

14. Ibid.

15. Cyril F. Brickfield, "Retirement, Work, and Lifelong Learning," Hearing Before the Special Committee on Aging, United States Senate, Nineth-fifth Congress Second Session (Washington, D.C.: U. S. Government Printing Office, 1978), p. 243.

16. Lamb and Duffy, op. cit., p. 17.

17. "It's Never Too Early to Plan," op. cit., p. 55.

18. Quoted in Lamb and Duffy, op. cit., p. 23.

19. "It's Never Too Early to Plan," op. cit., p. 56.

20. Louis Harris and Associates, Inc., *1979 Study of American Attitudes Toward Pension and Retirement* (New York: Johnson Higgins, 1979), p. viii.

21. Boyack, op. cit., p. 60.

22. Father Congreve, in *Concise Dictionary of Religious Quotations,* William Neil, ed. (Grand Rapids, Mich.: Wm. B. Eerdmans Publishing Company, 1974), p. 122.

3
Navigating the Mid-Life Storm

At middle age the soul should be opening up like a rose, not closing like a cabbage.

JOHN ANDREW HOLMES

Before beginning any new venture it is important to get our thoughts in order. That's why the next three chapters deal with the important matter of how we *think about* ourselves and our futures. Gaining a proper perspective on the second half of life is crucial, simply because our actions stem from our attitudes. The Bible says, "As [a man] thinketh in his heart, so is he . . ." (Proverbs 23:7 KJV).

There is probably no period in adult life when our attitudes about ourselves and life in general are shaken more than during the "threshold years" to life's second half—roughly, the late 30s and early 40s. It is during these years that so many men and women experience one of the most serious transitions in life, one that profoundly affects their futures—especially their ability to enjoy the retirement years. I'm referring, of course, to what is popularly called the "mid-life crisis." It's a subject that's receiving a good deal of attention today—and rightly so.

Barbara Fried, author of *The Middle Age Crisis,* says that "In our youth oriented society, childhood gets a lot of loving attention, old age is viewed with terror—and middle age is simply ignored."[1] Fortunately, that attitude is changing: our society is beginning to try to understand—and help tackle—some of the problems and challenges facing middle-agers.

What Is the Mid-Life Crisis?

Gail Sheehy, in her bestselling book *Passages,* defines this period as a stage in adult development—an adult "life passage."[2] It's one of many such passages, each a unique stage of emotional development and growth, with which each of us can easily identify.

Most authorities identify the period between 18 and 22 as one in which we "pull up roots." Going away to college, military service, or even away-from-home employment, we begin to stretch out beyond the security and restrictions of home. And in doing so, we begin to establish our own unique identity.

In our twenties, we begin to deal with the responsibilities of life—marriage, children, careers, a home. The searching questions that began with "Why" during our teenage years have now changed to *"How* do I begin?" . . . *"What* do I need?" . . . *"Where* can I go for help?"

The early thirties are a period of growing independence and vitality—as well as a period of putting down deeper roots. Of necessity, we challenge some of the "shoulds" as we begin to form our own value systems and begin to build a more independent family unit.

In his book *Men in Mid-Life Crisis,* Jim Conway says that, in the early thirties, "Life becomes less provisional. The husband makes deeper commitments, takes on more adult responsibilities, invests more of himself in family and personal interests, and within this framework, pursues long-range plans and goals.

"During this second settling-down period, a man continues to build his nest, at the same time pursuing with great ambition the dreams and goals of his life. During this highly active period, he has little time for reflection on the purpose of what he is doing."[3]

The Questioning Years

This last characteristic seems to act almost as a "pressure cooker," which—in the late 30s and early 40s—begins to release its energy, either slowly or explosively. This "energy" usually is manifested in the form of a strong, unsettling desire to break out of the life structure of the past and present. It is a period accompanied by questions such as, "Is what I'm doing right for the real me?" . . . "Do I really want to continue doing something that all of a sudden seems so dull and meaningless?" . . . Even "What is the real purpose of my life?" Such questions reveal not only an anxiety for meaning in life, but sometimes also new doubts about previously held convictions and goals.

> It is common to feel alone in the middle years, to wonder if your job is what you want, if the role you have accepted is still valid, and if your marriage will last. It is easy to be angry at God, life, and family; to be tired of achieving; to be *sick* of acting responsibly.[4]

Popular columnist Erma Bombeck has said, "Forty is God's punishment for our not having tithed." The theology is a bit warped, but much about the 40s *can* seem like "punishment."

This kind of inner conflict is bound to be unsettling, to say the least. And one thing that makes it that way is the difficulty of defining exactly what we're feeling, and why. The crisis, therefore, becomes one of "ambivalence and uncertainty, a time when we tend to feel bored, dissatisfied, restless, hemmed in by life, and plagued by an unscratchable, free-floating itch."[5] Of course, dissatisfaction breeds unpredictability. One day, a middle-aged Santayana is supposed to have said to a class of Yale undergraduates, "Gentlemen, it is spring." After which remark he put on his coat and hat and left, never to return.

This "unscratchable, free-floating itch" does have its points of origin, however.

The Point of No Return

Mid-life represents the halfway point. From age 20 to 40, many things were accomplished, with great effort: the establishing of a home, a family, a career. Now, with many of those goals attained—and some still unattained—we are face to face with the fact that youth (supposedly our "best years") has passed us by. We used to think we had forever and a day. Now we realize we don't.

This sense of "loss" is very real during mid-life.

> A man is facing the death of his physical prowess, in the sense that he is no longer a young man; death of the visions and ambitions of his teens and twenties; death of his hopes and aspirations for great achievement and advancement;

death of his sexual fantasies; death of the visions for fame
and fortune; death for some of the expectation he has had
for his children. Yes, and for the first time, he is facing the
reality of his own physical death.[6]

For many, the first visible indication of this period comes
when they look in the mirror. At middle age, the exterior of
our physical "temple," no matter how carefully maintained,
begins to crumble and sag. As someone has said: "I have everything I used to have—except now it's all one inch lower."

A woman sees the first streaks of gray in her hair . . . or begins
to talk with her doctor about the need for estrogen replace-
ment . . . or someone points out that her daughter is becoming
a young woman. As one woman put it in *The Middle Age Crisis*:
"Everything that makes life worth living for me is either turning gray, drying up, or leaving home."

The Angry Adolescent

However, this sense of loss runs deeper than the objective
realities of losing one's hair, or seeing children leave the nest.
It is really an identity crisis very much akin to another period
of life. Many psychoanalysts describe the revolt of the middle-
aged man as an "emotional second adolescence":

> Where 40 and 14 differ, of course, is that this is the sec-
> ond time around for the adult; what he is involved in is not
> so much a quest for identity as an inquest. His identity
> conflicts express the fact that he is overhauling, from his
> middle-aged vantage point, precisely that series of social
> and personal commitments that he chose to give meaning
> to his life 20 odd years before. . . . As one unhappy 40s said,
> "Sure I feel trapped. Why shouldn't I? Twenty-five years
> ago a dopey 18-year-old college kid made up his mind that
> I was going to be a dentist. So now here I am, a dentist. I'm
> stuck. What I want to know is, who told the kid he could
> decide what I was going to do for the rest of my life?"[7]

In today's society, two of the most visible manifestations of
this "adolescent" search for identity are *career changes* and
marital boredom and infidelity.

Career Change

Sit down and consider for a moment how many of your acquaintances have made major career changes in their early or mid-40s. (In fact, one of these people could be you!)

Jeffrey Sonnenfeld, writing in *The Harvard Business Review,* said that ". . . there has been an outstanding peak in job mobility for those in their mid-30s to mid-40s. . . . Candidates for second careers tend to be in their 40s and report a *perceived discrepancy between personal aspirations and current opportunities* for achievement and promotion" (italics added).[8]

It is common for a middle-aged person to reevaluate his ideas about his job or profession. Often, work that was once important now seems meaningless; senseless. The question "Why?" or "What for?" crops up constantly. Of course, such questions can paralyze initiative and wreak havoc with creativity and productivity. Even preconceived ideas of "success" can sour in a new desire to make life count for something beyond the weekly paycheck and the empty kudos that trickle down from management.

Herb Barks, author of *Prime Time,* says, "At middle-age we are very vulnerable to the emotions of unrest and the desire to change, until one day we finally say, 'It is not enough; there must be more. I want my share. I want ecstasy. Who said I had to be sentenced to this unhappy situation forever? I want what I deserve—a little abandon, a little kicking off of my shoes. I am tired of achieving, of being super-responsible. I want to think about me.' "[9]

Rightly used, this kind of conflict can become the stuff out of which great decisions are made. The realization that time is passing by and that opportunities for new starts in life are coming to an end has brought new determination and creativity to many a man and woman in their 40s. The stories of new ventures and careers launched during mid-life are well-documented—though so are the stories of failure and disappointment stemming from hasty decisions born more of emotional frustration than wisdom.

Unfortunately, any time of confusion, unsettledness, or crisis provides an easy entry point for the enemy of our souls. Jesus said that "the thief" (Satan) comes only to "steal, . . . kill, and . . . destroy" (John 10:10 KJV). That's the "bottom line" of his every effort and activity. And that activity is especially evident during crises . . . whether a family crisis or a vocational one, a young person's adolescent agonies or the mid-life crisis of a troubled adult.

C. S. Lewis wrote in *The Screwtape Letters:* "The long, dull, monotonous years of middle-aged prosperity or middle-aged adversity are excellent campaigning weather [for the devil]. . . ."[10]

Target: Marriage

One of the major battle "campaigns" often takes place in the arena of the marriage relationship. For the husband, youth, virility, even meaning in life seem to be slipping away, yielding to a restless anxiety for something more, something better, something *new.* And deep within that anxiety lies the need for reassurance and reaffirmation.

Many times, that need shows itself in the form of increasing pressure on the *other* partner in the marriage to change and become more "considerate," more "affectionate" . . . perhaps more "romantic." The resulting tensions can usually be resolved in those unions where there is deep commitment and open communication between husband and wife. However, far too often today this search for reassurance leaps the bounds of the marriage and seeks fulfillment in an illicit affair. Even divorce can loom as "the" solution, with the new partner seen as "the" person needed to help bring out the "new me."

The problem is that neither an affair nor divorce can deliver the goods. The short-lived ecstasy of a new relationship doesn't create a "new you." It is only a dangerous detour, leaving the survivors (including, sometimes, entire families) even deeper in frustration and conflict.

A quote from "Oliver" says it well: "We were strangers looking into each other's eyes and seeing only ourselves. For awhile these mirrors gave back enhanced images, and we proclaimed our love for the bearer of the mirror; but the intimacy was an illusion."[11]

And to quote Barks again:

The affair, the other man, the other woman—they all reflect this image crisis because what a person seeks is not another person, but the image of themselves in the face of someone new. It is as if we think we can be reborn because someone else sees us as manly or seductive or beautiful or funny. This is why the affair itself is not fulfilling. The other person can reflect for awhile some image we need, but it will not be enough. Somehow the crisis of middle age must be met where it truly is—in ourselves, in our own lack of proper self-concept.[12]

That is where the problem is . . . and that is where the solution lies.

Look Inside—Not Outside

When you stop and think about it, what is it that gives us our self-concept—our sense of individual identity? Is it the beliefs and values traceable to our upbringing, our culture, our personal faith in God? Is it our sense of physical strength; virility; beauty; youth? Is it the sense of prestige or social rank due to our career? Is it the totality of our hopes and dreams of attaining success, reaching our goals . . . someday? Is it the hopes and dreams we have for our children—for *their* happiness and achievement?

For most of us, I think, our sense of identity and self-worth is bound up in how we feel about all of these things—and more.

But what happens when, at 36 or 42 or 48 years of age, we wake up one morning and discover we have some doubts about those old beliefs and convictions? What happens when the old answers don't seem to work for the questions we're facing now? What happens when we begin to have doubts about the validity of our job—about the importance of what we do—and, therefore, about who we are?

What happens when we look in the mirror and see gray hair and wrinkles, and stand face to face at last with something called "aging"? What happens when we come to the sudden conclusion that we've not accomplished what we thought we would by this time? What happens when we see the "perfect plans" we had for the kids not turning out so perfectly? What happens then?

It doesn't help for someone to tell us, blandly, "Friend,

you're just in mid-life crisis," because we feel like life is coming apart! And, in one sense, it is!

What's happening is that the images that have always helped us identify ourselves—the images that have always helped us "place" ourselves—are coming apart. And it's no wonder we feel like we're in a thousand pieces, floating in a thousand directions.

However, what we have to do is look closer, because something else is happening: *something new is being formed.*

God Is Rebuilding Us—for a Purpose

God knew we would reach this point in life: He arrived first . . . and it's just like a loving God to turn "the worst" into "the best." It is at this very time in our lives when God wants to put us in closer touch with the real source of our well-being, our worthwhileness, our identity. *He wants to liberate us from a self-concept so firmly shackled to the externals—to things, things that change and decay—and to bind our identity closer to His unchanging, unconditional love.*

If you find yourself experiencing the agonies described in this chapter—firsthand, now—this is where you can take heart. God's love is probably no stranger to you: you've understood it . . . you've no doubt made His love your own. But at this point of your life you have the opportunity to see that love (and yourself) in an entirely new way—and that's exactly the way God planned it!

But how does this love "become operational"—how does it "go to work on" your confusion, your "lostness"?

God's transforming love in Christ becomes dynamic—"begins working"—when it touches the point of your need. That's the ignition point. That's where the life and love of Jesus begin to happen!

Jesus dealt with this problem very clearly. "Only those who admit they are sick will get a doctor." Therefore, one of the central blocks to receiving love is our fear of showing weakness and need. At mid-life we are supposed to be the providers, to be adequate and mature. We may be all of those things, but we can still be painfully needy and never become free enough to say it. If I could identify one road

sign on the way to a better life at middle age, it would be
the one that says, "Face where you are. Admit first to God,
and then to selected others, your pain and your hurt."[13]

I urge you to do that now—today. Admit your need. *Then let
God love you.* Let Him show you that you are a worthy person
—a very special person in His sight. Accept that fact now, and
begin walking in the light of its reality.

And remember, God doesn't stop at just loving us: What the
Lord loves, He redeems. Past failures, mistakes, sins, broken
relationships, painful memories—all we have done (and failed
to do) the Lord forgives, and He actively works in our lives to
bring good out of seeming failure.

> Bless the Lord, O my soul, and forget none of His be-
> nefits; Who pardons all your iniquities; Who heals all your
> diseases; Who redeems your life from the pit; Who crowns
> you with lovingkindness and compassion; Who satisfies
> your years with good things, So that your youth is renewed
> like the eagle.
>
> Psalms 103:2–5 NAS

From the beginning of time God made provisions for this
point in your life. He knew you would need new equipment
and a new perspective for the second half of life.

You're at the close of a chapter of life all right . . . but for an
excellent reason:

So you can begin a new one!

Entering a New Day

Can there possibly be *benefits* to the mid-life crisis? Yes, and
they can be rich beyond calculation!

> The man who successfully navigates the mid-life crisis
> will experience an increase in productivity, a decrease in
> competitiveness, a greater desire to be helpful to people,
> the ability to enjoy leisure, and the ability to be alone. His
> marriage will generally become more meaningful and satis-
> fying to both partners. There will be an easy transition to
> becoming a grandparent and trainer of a new generation.[14]

But to experience the benefits, you must dare to risk. You must risk letting God love you in your need—then risk moving into new areas of experience and growth. If the deeper questions are settled, if you know where your true security and identity lie, now *may be* the right time to launch that new career you've always dreamed about, or learn that hobby or sport you've always wanted to tackle.

Properly understood, mid-life *is* the time to break out of ruts. It is the time for new interests . . . new relationships . . . new ministry to others. More than anything else, it's the time to take the risk of giving.

A chorus by Gloria Gaither sums it up for me:

> I am loved, I am loved,
> I can risk loving you,
> For the One who knows me best
> Loves me most.[15]

There's a post-mid-life-crisis song for you! There's a beginning-the-second-half anthem for us all!

It's a song for you. He's given you His love for such a time as this. And what He's given . . . receive.

I waited patiently for the Lord;
And He inclined to me, and heard my cry.
He brought me up out of the pit of destruction, out
  of the miry clay;
And He set my feet upon a rock making my footsteps firm.
And He put a new song in my mouth, a song of praise
  to our God:
Many will see and fear,
And will trust in the Lord.

Psalms 40:1–3 NAS

Source Notes

1. Barbara Fried, *The Middle Age Crisis* (New York: Harper and Row Publishers, Inc., 1967), p. 1.
2. Gail Sheehy, *Passages* (New York: E. P. Dutton, 1976), pp. 29, 46.
3. Jim Conway, *Men in Mid-Life Crisis* (Elgin, Ill.: David C.

Cook Publishing Company, 1978), p. 141.

4. Herb Barks, *Prime Time—Moving into Middle Age with Style* (Nashville, Tenn.: Thomas Nelson, Inc., 1978), p. 14.
5. Fried, op. cit., p. 6.
6. Conway, op. cit., p. 145.
7. Fried, op. cit., p. 59.
8. Jeffrey Sonnenfeld, "Dealing With the Aging Work Force," *Harvard Business Review,* November-December 1978, p. 83.
9. Barks, op. cit., p. 70.
10. C. S. Lewis, in *Concise Dictionary of Religious Quotations,* William Neil, ed. (Grand Rapids, Mich.: William B. Eerdmans Publishing Company, 1974), p. 118.
11. Quoted in Fried, op. cit., p. 109.
12. Barks, op. cit., p. 17.
13. Ibid., p. 120.
14. Conway, op. cit., p. 142.
15. William J. and Gloria Gaither, "I Am Loved," Gaither Music Publishers, 1978.

4
Thinking Straight About Aging

To know how to grow old is the masterwork of wisdom, and one of the most difficult chapters in the great art of living.

HENRI FREDERIC AMIEL

The fear of aging is probably the greatest hindrance to enjoying life's second half. Not only is it a burden that no human being was created to carry, but—like so many of our fears—it is self-fulfilling. Medical experts agree that a lifetime sown with fearful thoughts about aging inevitably bears a harvest of emotional and physical affliction.

The curious thing is that most of our fears about aging are based upon unfounded myths that have either been passed down to us from previous generations or are erroneously accepted as facts in our intensely youth-oriented society.

A fulfilling retirement demands that we rid our minds forever of these myths. However, to do this we need to know what aging is (and what it is not), and to understand just why the familiar errors about aging are relentlessly promoted as truth.

Young America

There is something about our country that has always made us obsessed with youth. In saying this, I'm not talking about a healthy admiration for the young people of our nation: I'm all for that. No, what I'm talking about is our seeming national obsession with being young forever!

Perhaps it goes back in our history to the fact that our forefathers broke away from cultural and social settings entrenched in traditions dating back hundreds, even thousands, of years. When they came to this country, they created something completely new—blazing new trails, carving a nation out of a wilderness, creating a new republic built upon inventiveness, adaptation, flexibility, and productivity.

But somewhere along the line, something got mixed up. We began equating all of these admirable qualities with youth—as if they were one and the same.

> The Chinese, for example, equate age with wisdom. They value who you are more than what you do. In our society we tend to reverse the order. We value productivity, not the quality of life, and we are drawn more and more to a worship of youth.[1]

At first glance, this worship of youth seems essentially harmless.

> Yet it has its seamier side. One outgrowth of the nation's aversion to aging has been a tendency to look askance at, and often down on, people in the later years of life.[2]

This, in turn, has created a "youth cult" mentality that tends to pressure the populus to do everything it can to *stop* the aging process.

. . . Of the Young, by the Young, for the Young

Nowhere is this mentality more blatantly revealed than in our consumer advertising. We are continually reminded "by the standards for beauty, by the fashions and clothes and hair styles, that it's infinitely better to be young and foolish than to be anything else."[3] The products offered to meet this national need for youth are unlimited: diets, lotions, wrinkle removers, plastic surgery, beauty preparations made from exotic plants and insects ("natural," don't you see), face-lifts, exercise salons. Men are told that they can "take off years" by dying their hair, concealing baldness with a wig, or wearing clothes that, to an increasing degree, are designed to look good only on the very slim and trim—that is to say, the young.

What all of this adds up to is a cultural need to *deny our aging* and its physiological effects. The message is that if you use this or that product you will never "grow old." As one frustrated middle-ager said to me, "We're being programmed to be 25 years old all our lives!"

To Deny It Is to Fear It

Of course, by the very fact of trying to deny aging we are admitting our fear of it.

> Many Americans suffer from what R. O. Bechman, who is affiliated with the Senior Service Foundation in Miami, Florida, calls gerontophobia, or the fear of growing old. . . . Indeed a State University of New York survey found that 40% of Americans dread growing old. So intense is this fear in many younger people in the U.S., Dr. Bechman says, that they shun or ignore the aged.[4]

It is this phobic reaction to aging that is so clearly reflected in the media.

In a previous chapter we pointed out that many of these attitudes are changing. One reason for this is that, today, nearly 25 million Americans—or approximately 11.2 percent of the total population—are over 65, and the proportion of people in that age bracket is rising all the time. The influence of this increase in the number of middle-aged Americans is having a significant impact upon our nation's attitude toward aging.

Unfortunately, however, all our lives you and I have been bombarded by the propaganda of a culture that says: "Young is good—old is bad." And, though we might not have thought about it, our thinking is pretty well permeated with that message.

It's Called "Ageism"

> Ageism existed, of course, long before the word for it. It works like other isms. Racism takes skin color as a determining sign of personality and character traits. Just so, ageism consists of taking a mere count of years as a sure gauge of somebody's capacity and vitality.[5]

In his book *Life's Second Half,* Jerome Ellison has a chapter entitled "Our Strange Tribal Rites." One of those "rites" deals with a very obvious attitude of ageism, which Ellison describes as the rite or ritual of "shunning." In many primitive tribes, it seems, a person found guilty of a serious crime is ostracized from the tribe. Many times, the person soon becomes ill and dies. His reason for living has been taken from him.

Ellison goes on to say that we, too, use shunning in our society as punishment for crimes—the most common of which, by *our* tribal definition, is aging! Ellison points out that, once a person is considered "old," the following happens:

> Immediate and drastic social retaliation—shunning—is promptly invoked. Whatever the presumed benefits to the tribe, the damage to the guilty individuals is calamitous, particularly among males.[6]

However, there is another aspect of our "tribal tradition" that is equally destructive—the cruel caricature of the aged in cartoons, movies, and television commercials. Representative Claude Pepper, Chairman of the House Committee on Aging, said during a recent hearing:

> In the real world, older women do not hide toilet paper in their purses, offer strangers "tummy" remedies, or mistake factory-produced foods for their own homemade goods. We need to ask why "younger" is a positive term and "older" a pejorative one in televised ads, whether it is necessary to ridicule an older man's deafness in order to sell lemonade, and why older women are often caricatured or portrayed as incompetent in commercials.[7]

The important thing to understand is that this caricature is more than just unkind and cruel: it is also unwarranted and unfounded. If the facts are left to themselves, aging presents a far different picture than that presented in the media—or, for that matter, in our casual humor about "old folks."

What Is Aging?

Even experts have difficulty saying what aging really is. Even they cannot cleanly separate the social, behavioral, and biological changes that we look upon as aging from those changes that are the result of medical history, cultural and ethnic settings, the manner of a person's life-style, and other externals. This means that, for generations, we have made an arbitrary division between middle age and "old age" at about 60 years old. The result is that most people are conditioned to accept a set of beliefs about their aging. After a particular age, they *expect* their intellectual capability, their memory, and their capacity to adapt to change to deteriorate. Similarly, they *expect* to be vulnerable to certain diseases and physical disorders.

However, the truth is that, in general, older people respond readily to changing circumstances, because of a greater fund of patience and experience, and a mature perspective on life. Studies show also that older people do not have more mental disorders than the young: senility, for example, is not an inevitable condition of aging, but rather is often caused by the fear of it.[8]

Intelligence Can Increase With Age

As a result of research done in the '30s, we have long thought that intelligence reached a peak at about age 25, held to a high plateau for about 10 years, and then slowly declined.[9] For more than a generation, this appraisal has been regarded as an unalterable fact. However:

> A long series of recent studies, conducted by K. Warren Schaie, Paul B. Bates, and associates in the United States and confirmed by sociologists in Germany, have demonstrated beyond any question that the most important factors of intelligence continue to increase well into the 70s, and, if certain simple conditions are met, throughout life.[10]

According to an article in the *Harvard Business Review*, when time pressure is not a relevant factor, the performance of older people tends to be as good as—if not better than—that of younger people. "Recent researchers have . . . found problem solving, number facility and verbal comprehension to be unaffected by age. The ability to find and apply general rules to problem solving are more related to an individual's flexibility and education than to age."[11]

As for senility, gerontologists agree that it is but a layman's term used by the general public (and some doctors who should know better) to categorize the behavior of the old. True, some of what is called senility is caused by brain damage; however, most of the actions and behavior that, collectively, we call senility are caused by personal frustration, anxiety, depression, and other problems that are not only treatable but reversible.

You Can Stay Flexible

As for inflexibility, Dr. Robert N. Butler has written:

> The ability to change and adapt has little to do with one's age, and more to do with one's lifelong character. . . . The notion that older people become less responsive to innovation is not supported by scientific studies of healthy older people living in the community or by everyday observations and clinical psychiatric experience.[12]

You Can Be "Fit As a Fiddle"

No one would deny that age normally brings with it an overall loss of physical strength. But again, the notion that chronic illness is the automatic accompaniment of age is false.

In this connection, I think of a friend, Frank Nederson, who for the past ten years has been keeping himself in shape and preparing for retirement by jogging for twenty minutes each morning from room to room in his house. Now, at 65, he has just scaled mountain peak #274 from the Southern California Sierra Club peak list (a "peak" being between four and five thousand feet). Here is a man, incidentally, who would never consider himself an "athlete": his career, for one thing, was forged in management and personnel. However, he has always been serious about his diet and physical conditioning, and about not letting his age automatically determine his physical well-being.

And Frank's numbers, I'm delighted to tell you, are growing!

Sexual Potency

With the multiplicity of recent articles and testimonials affirming the continued sexual potency of the aged, it's unlikely that anyone continues to doubt the fact. And again, such problems as do occur seem often to have more to do with fear than reality.

> Men consider that their sexual powers are on the downgrade, become morbidly preoccupied with approaching age, and resign themselves to prostate troubles, urinary disturbances, heart troubles and even cancer of various organs that they believe to be imminent. The radius of their fear increases; the other organs are engulfed. The end result is a typical hypochondriacal picture.[13]

In 1974, Hermon Brotman of the Department of Health, Education and Welfare said that each year in America there are some 35,000 marriages of persons above age 64, and that "sex as well as companionship and economy are given as the reasons."[14] There is every reason to believe that the numbers have done nothing but increase since then, with the motivations no doubt staying about the same.

Oliver Wendell Holmes, Jr., may just have summed it up when, at 92, he saw a pretty girl and said, "What I wouldn't give to be 70 again!"[15]

In spite of the twisted picture we have of the foibles of aging, the simple facts are on the side of a healthy, productive and fulfilling second half. The bottom line, as Frank Trippett puts it, is that ageism is a "patchwork of prejudices and predispositions" that will not be banished by any sort of official edict. No, "It will remain for individuals to prove, by the sheer living of life, that habitual beliefs about the meaning of age are often at variance with the truths of the heart."[16]

Age Has the Advantage

Those "truths of the heart" referred to above tell us that aging can actually open the door to a new dimension of living. Aging lets us enjoy some of the insights, values, and wisdom we lacked—or tended to ignore—in our earlier years. Because we have by now had the experience of making mistakes—and, it's to be hoped, learning from them—we often have a greater tolerance of others, which in turn leads to a greater ability to love and understand.

> [We can even] perceive that youth, so publicized as allur-
> ing and perfect, in reality is often merely an interval of
> elementary learning, a rather hard prep school . . . whereas
> the *second* half of life can in point of fact be enriched with
> genuine appreciation and achievement. At least 90 percent
> of humanity's grandeur has been wrought by persons past
> 35 years of age; much of it by people past 70.[17]

Gandhi was 72 when he led India's independence movement. Grandma Moses didn't begin painting until she was 74. Jomo Kenyatta was in his 70s when he became the first president of the African Republic of Kenya. Albert Schweitzer lectured around the globe on the brotherhood of man when he was in his 80s. Bertrand Russell, one of the most influential thinkers of the twentieth century, was 90 when he intervened with heads of state during the Cuban missile crisis. On his 82nd birthday, Arthur Fiedler confessed, "Oh yes, I am slowing a little. Until a short time ago I was conducting 194 concerts a year. That was too many, so now I have cut them down to 164 a year."[18] Agatha Christie was writing her world-famous mystery novels right up to the time of her death, well into her 80s. Gladstone wrote some of his finest works in his 60s and 70s. Ben Franklin was a world-renowned diplomat in his 70s. That great man of faith, George Mueller of Bristol, England, was still working in his 90s. Hudson Taylor was working until his retirement only four years before his death at 83. Bismarck, Lloyd George, Winston Churchill, Clemenceau, Douglas MacArthur, and a host of others were creative and active right into their 80s and 90s. And, if that's not enough for you, consider that Michelangelo *began* his architectural work on St. Peter's Church at age 76!

And They're Everywhere

At the same time, consider some of the not-so-famous people of our world—people you never read about in the national magazines, but who represent millions of "the aged" who are both tremendously productive and still getting a very big kick out of life.

Seventy-year-old Sing Lum is a realtor in Bakersfield, California. He retired from farming ten years ago, but said, "I couldn't just sit around. After three or four months, I went back to school."[19] He earned his real-estate license, and in 1979 had a half-million dollars in listings. (By the way, he also holds several world track records for men in his age group.)

Dr. Hal Marquis, age 71, is a retired cardiologist who keeps busy attending West Valley College in San Jose, California. Marquis began his "retirement" by going back to medical school to take a brush-up course. So did his wife, Mary, who is a nurse. Besides being enrolled in a "wide range of classes that give him the chance for new experiences," Hal and his wife have been active in raising support for the building of a hospital in Guatemala.[20]

Sister Emmanuel Ferron was recently given a special farewell reception at Saint Joseph's Medical Center in Burbank, California. Her nursing career ended in 1963 at the age of 63. She then promptly began her "new career" as supervisor of this very busy hospital's mail room. (However, she *is* retiring now—at age 80!)[21]

Seventy-one-year-old Albert Krone was interviewed recently at a meeting of the Western Gerontological Society at the Disneyland Hotel in Anaheim, California. His comments: "Listen, I'm a senior citizen. I'm retired. But I am not an old person." His friend Josephine Repass, age 73, joined in: "Well, now, I'm not young, but I try not to let myself think I'm old. I just go on as if I were 20." Both are busy in advocacy workshops for senior citizens.[22]

You should also know about an organization working in connection with the Los Angeles Unified School District's Volunteer and Tutorial Program called "Dedicated Older Volunteers in Educational Services," or DOVES. There are some 3,200 DOVES working in Los Angeles schools, as vocational counselors, assistants to classroom teachers and librarians, and seminar moderators, and in other activities (including meeting with young people and exposing them to people from the real world of work). DOVES include people like Edward Fair, 59, a retired school teacher; Jack Grodsky, 66, a retired baker; Jacob Bischin, 78, a former department store buyer; Harold

Greenspan, 74, a retired stockbroker; and Clara Den, 73, a retired bank teller.[23]

The reason for listing these examples is not so much to promote the importance of meaningful activity after retirement: we'll get to that later. Rather, it is to introduce a few people who, though they are certainly among the "elderly," are daily placing significant demands upon their minds and bodies, performing very valuable services to their fellow men—*and* having the time of their lives doing it!

Incidentally, the fact that these few examples are all from the Southern California area reveals nothing more than just that that's where I call home. And, remember, these are just a handful of the tens of thousands of older citizens in my area whose minds are bright and whose bodies are strong. Think of the thousands in *your* area—and of the millions across the country. They are the "proof of the pudding." Their lives argue eloquently against the mythological claims about aging.

"But How Can I Make Sure I'm One of Them?"

I'll guarantee you that all of the people listed above have one thing in common: a healthy attitude toward aging. For years, each one of them invested in that right attitude, and now they are reaping the dividends.

And preparing for aging *is* like making an investment:

> The people with whom we associate, the books and magazines we read, the television programs we watch, the music to which we listen, the thoughts with which we fill our minds—all of these mold our attitudes toward life as we grow older. In the end we are the sum total of our earlier choices.[24]

But it is vitally important to make those choices *now*. It is important to invest in a healthy mind-set and healthy attitudes *now*. Remember, what you will be, you are now becoming.

Accept Your Aging

The first big step in building this healthy attitude is to accept the fact that each of us is getting older every day. Even if you're only 35 or 40, now is the time to begin "living with" this reality. The creams, diets, and "mod" clothes might make you look nicer (?) and even bolster your ego, but they won't keep you from aging inside them.

To deny aging is to fear it. And, once we concede that fear is generally self-fulfilling, we know that there really is "nothing to fear [about aging] except fear itself."

I think of my friend, Dr. Herbert Lockyer, the world-renowned Bible lecturer, whose life and ministry continue to be a blessing at 93 years of age. Listen to what he says:

> Benjamin Disraeli must have had a chip on his shoulder when he wrote in *Coningsby:* "Youth is a blunder; manhood a struggle; old age a regret." Since I have passed my 93rd milestone on life's pilgrimage (I was born on September 10, 1886), I am a living lie to old age being a regret. Certainly, as I look back over past years, I have many regrets; but I have no distress of mind over being an old man. I am deliciously satisfied and contented, in spite of the fact that I am now "old and grayheaded," as the Psalmist expresses it, and am daily proving that "godliness with contentment is great gain."[25]

Accepting the fact of aging—and what is more, enjoying it —will free enormous amounts of emotional energy, energy that can be channeled into new relationships and activities. On the other hand, denying the fact of aging *consumes* enormous amounts of emotional energy, because such denial is counter to the very purposes of God, and thus to the natural flow of life.

Now One Step Further—How About Being Thankful?

For the Christian, there is an even more positive and active form of the principle of acceptance. It is called *thankfulness.*

The Bible says that we are to let the peace of Christ rule in our hearts and "be *thankful*" (Colossians 3:15, italics added). Paul says, "In everything give *thanks;* for this is God's will for you in Christ Jesus" (1 Thessalonians 5:18 NAS, italics added). We are also encouraged to "Be anxious for nothing [aging perhaps?], but in everything by prayer and supplication with thanksgiving let your requests be made known to God" (Philippians 4:6 NAS).

Thankfulness is so very important because it brings into our lives the very ingredient most needed. It is called *peace*—that peace of mind and heart that brings wholeness and rest to our jangled lives. But peace will never be obtained by denying our age—or our aging—in a frantic search for the fountain of youth. No, peace comes when we are thankful for who we are in Christ, and who we are becoming . . . *year* by precious *year.* The benefit is ". . . the peace of God, which surpasses all comprehension, [which] shall guard your hearts and your minds in Christ Jesus" (Philippians 4:6, 7 NAS).

The Bible reveals abundant provision at every stage of life —and there's good reason to be thankful!

> Surely goodness and lovingkindness will follow me *all the days* of my life, and I will dwell in the house of the Lord forever.
>
> Psalms 23:6 NAS, italics added

> But the godly shall flourish like palm trees, and grow tall as the cedars of Lebanon. For they are transplanted into the Lord's own garden, and are under his personal care. Even in old age they will still produce fruit and be vital and green.
>
> Psalms 92:12–14 LB

> I will be your God through all your lifetime, yes, even when your hair is white with age. I made you and I will care for you. I will carry you along and be your Savior.
>
> Isaiah 46:4 LB

Thankfulness Brings Transformation

Being thankful for God's gift of life—including every phase of aging—will bring transformation. Genuine thankfulness is an outward expression and witness of an inner trust in the goodness and provision of a loving God. That's why thankfulness is so important—and so dynamic!

The Apostle Paul says, "Do not be conformed to this world, but be transformed by the renewing of your mind, that you may prove what the will of God is, that which is good and acceptable and perfect" (Romans 12:2 NAS). The Living Bible translates this: "Then you will learn from your own experience how his ways will really satisfy you."

We know how our culture approaches aging: "Old is bad . . . young is good." Aging is to be feared . . . youthfulness is to be craved, if not worshipped. If this is our thinking, we are conforming to a system of thought that brings only more fear —and with it, emotional and physical affliction.

But Jesus said, ". . . I came that they might have life, and might have it abundantly" (John 10:10 NAS). Notice that that promise contains no age restrictions. Abundant life does not have to stop at age 40, or 60, or 80!

Abundant life is the reward of those who are thankful for life's every season . . . thankful for the past . . . thankful for the present . . . and thankful for the future—including that part of it called aging!

Be thankful . . . and be transformed!

Grow old along with me!
The best is yet to be,
The last of life, for which the first was made;
Our times are in His hand
Who saith "A whole I planned,
Youth shows but half; trust God: see all, nor be afraid!"[26]

Source Notes

1. Jim Conway, *Men in Mid-Life Crisis* (Elgin, Ill.: David C. Cook Publishing Company, 1978), p. 51.
2. Frank Trippett, "Time Essay: Looking Askance at Ageism," *Time,* March 24, 1980, p. 88.
3. Barbara Fried, *The Middle Age Crisis* (New York: Harper and Row Publishers, Inc., 1967), p. 77.
4. Lee Butcher, *Retirement Without Fear* (Princeton, N.J.: Dow Jones Books, 1978), p. 71.
5. Trippett, op. cit., p. 88.
6. Jerome Ellison, *Life's Second Half* (Old Greenwich, Conn.: The Devin-Adair Co., Inc. 1978), p. 14.
7. Quoted in Paul Friggens, "Don't Call Me Senior Citizen," *The Rotarian,* March 1979, p. 17.
8. Reuel L. Howe, *How to Stay Younger While Growing Older* (Waco, Tex.: Word, Inc., 1974), p. 149.
9. Ellison, op. cit., p. 17.
10. Ibid.

11. Jeffrey Sonnenfeld, "Dealing With the Aging Work Force," *Harvard Business Review,* November-December 1978.
12. Quoted in Friggens, op. cit., pp. 19, 50.
13. Fried, op. cit., p. 81.
14. Quoted in Alexander Leaf, "Every Day Is a Gift When You're Over 100," *National Geographic,* January 1974, p. 111.
15. Oliver Wendell Holmes, Jr., in *The Crown Treasury of Relevant Quotations,* Edward F. Murphy, ed. (New York: Crown Publishers, Inc., 1978), p. 22.
16. Trippett, op. cit., p. 88.
17. Oren Arnold, *The Second Half of Your Life* (Irvine, Calif.: Harvest House Pubs., Inc., 1979), p. 9.
18. Ibid., p. 74.
19. Joan Swenson, "Realtor Runs Rings Around Competition," *Bakersfield Californian,* March 30, 1980.
20. "Retiring Isn't Taking It Easy," *San Jose* (Calif.) *News,* April 1, 1980.
21. " 'Guardian Angel' Retiring at Age 80," *Burbank* (Calif.) *Daily Review,* February 14, 1980.
22. Elizabeth Mehren, "Gerontology: A Sturdy Stand for Elders," *Los Angeles Times,* March 12, 1980.
23. Norman Sklarewitz, "Is There Life After Retirement?" *California,* May 1979, p. 41.
24. Phillip Keller, quoted in Dr. Gary Collins, "How To Handle Aging," *Christian Herald,* March 1980.
25. Herbert Lockyer, "93 and Not Out," *Decision,* March 1980, p. 7.
26. Robert Browning, "Rabbi Ben Ezra," *The Complete Poetical Works of Robert Browning* (Boston: Houghton Mifflin Company, 1895).

5
Looking Death Square in the Eye

Is Death the last sleep? No, it is the last final awakening.

SIR WALTER SCOTT

There is no subject that can put us in touch with the meaning of our existence as swiftly as the fact of death.

Ever since the disobedience of Adam and Eve, death has been with us. Yet for most of us, the concept of death remains strange and distant. Death is something that somehow stands apart from reality. We don't even know how to talk about it or think about it, much less deal with it. Freud wrote: "No one believes in his own death. In the unconscious, everyone is convinced of his immortality."[1]

Facing the Unfamiliar

One reason for this is because, at least in our country, death is kept so very "unfamiliar." Death is treated as an "abnormal" part of our lives. It is isolated and kept apart from society. In his book *Denial of Death,* Dr. Ernest Becker feels this process of intentional isolation begins at a very early age:

> We routinely shelter children from death and dying, thinking we are protecting them from harm. But it is clear that we do them a disservice by depriving them of the experience. By making death and dying a taboo subject and keeping children away from the people who are dying or who have died we create a fear that need not be there. When a person dies, we "help" their loved ones by doing things for them, being cheerful and fixing up the body so it looks "natural."[2]

This process of denying the normalcy of death has increased as we've become more urbanized. Many of us who were raised on farms or rural areas came early into contact with the reality of reproduction, the pain and joy of birth, and the reality of death quite often, all of them during the course of a year. We learned to integrate the fact of death into living. Some of the animals we saw die were household pets—and, mourning them, we learned to cope with the emotions of permanent loss.

In addition, a generation or two ago, hospitals, doctors, and mortuaries weren't so easily accessible: more often than not, our relatives died at home. As children, there were fewer ways for us to be "scurried away" and "protected" from the fact of the death of a friend or relative. We had to deal with death as a normal part of life.

"Pretend It's Not There, and It Will Go Away"

America has long been a death-denying society. In fact, as we saw in the last chapter, ours is a society that has long tried to deny the aging process itself. This just isn't true in many other cultures. Elisabeth Kübler-Ross contrasts us with the Trukese of Micronesia, who she describes as a death-*affirming* society:

> We are reluctant to reveal our age; we spend fortunes to hide our wrinkles; we prefer to send our old people to nursing homes. For the Trukese, life ends when you are 40; death begins when you are 40.[3]

As stated in that one terse sentence, that view may seem morbid—the product of a "heathen" culture. But woven properly, as it is, into the fabric of a society that both welcomes and venerates the aged, the Trukese view seems to me to be more realistic and more compassionate than the death-defying charade staged by our society.

Our Personal Encounter

However, this cultural denial must in time give way to death's inevitability. Sooner or later, we must come to terms with this greatest of all our limitations.

For many of us, it begins at middle age. Because of an awakened realization to our own aging, it is often then that we begin to see our lives from a different perspective. Whereas before we used to see only a "forever future" before us, we now see our lives in terms of a life span with a definite beginning—and a just as definite ending. As never before, we begin to measure our existence in terms of "years left." Herb Barks says that when we admit we are middle-aged we have made a decision that "accepts the questionable fact that death has the right and the ability to place 'middle' upon [our] life."[4]

It is also at this point in life that death begins to become very personal. Those people who we thought would be "with us forever"—uncles, aunts, a mother, a father—begin to die. All too often, because of our unpreparedness, this confrontation with death is traumatic, and with the loss of a loved one we find ourselves face to face with one of the most profound facts of life—our own mortality.

The Sting

Experts agree, however, that the fact of death affects our lives long before any such crisis event:

> Behind the sense of insecurity and the face of danger, behind the sense of discouragement and depression, there always lurks the basic fear of death, a fear which undergoes most complex elaborations and manifests itself in many indirect ways. . . . No one is free of the fear of death. . . .[5]

Dr. Paul Tournier says that "All anxiety is reduced to anxiety about death. . . . Man carries death about within him all his life long, but it becomes more threatening as he grows old."[6] So death is more, then, than some feared physical event in the future.

The fear of death is destructive because it imposes a perverted view of life. First Corinthians 15:55 refers to the "sting of death." That "sting" is defined as the sin innate in humanity, which includes the entire principle of decay and brokenness that manifests itself in disease, in sickness, and in shattered and torn relationships. This "sting of death" also includes fear—the fear of death. In our culture, it exhibits itself in a herd-like mentality rushing forward in futility, trying to gain and have and experience all it can before the ruler of all—Death—delivers its final blow, against which no man has an appeal.

This inner time pressure doesn't have to be articulated, incidentally, to be at work. It is a silent thing that can be unspoken —even unconscious. Success must be gained quickly—while we're young. Material goods must be acquired and accumulated *now*, while they "can still be enjoyed." The clock is ticking . . . opportunity is slipping away. . . . there's only just so much time . . . "get it while you can. . . ."

After all is said and done, though, the culprit is death. And if death rules the consciousness, even preparation for retirement can be an anxious, fearful time—a frenzied reaction to the Final Limitation—death.

The question is, if physical death is inevitable, is there a way to subdue its power? The answer for Christians is, of course, yes. Death does not have to rule over us, because death with all its effects has already been subdued.

There are two principles that can help lead you to your personal "victory" over death—and, have a profound effect on your ability to enjoy your retirement years. One is your acceptance of the fact of physical death; the other is your acceptance of the fact of eternal life.

Accepting the Fact of Physical Death

Fortunately, the greatest of all books gives a balanced perspective to the most troubling of life's questions. With all of the Bible's emphasis upon the newness of life, on abundant life, on everlasting life, it never denies physical death. The Bible deals in reality. Thus, it says that ". . . we are sojourners before Thee, and tenants, as all our fathers were; our days on the earth are like a shadow . . ." (1 Chronicles 29:15 NAS). "No man has authority to restrain the wind with the wind, or authority over the day of death . . ." (Ecclesiastes 8:8 NAS). "Yet you do not know what your life will be like tomorrow. You are just a vapor that appears for a little while and then vanishes away" (James 4:14 NAS). ". . . it is appointed for men to die once, and after this comes judgment" (Hebrews 9:27 NAS).

The Bible accepts death as a fact and encourages us to do the same. Yet at the same time, it gives this seemingly paradoxical

—and thrilling—pronouncement: "Death is swallowed up in victory. O death, where is thy sting? O grave, where is thy victory?" (1 Corinthians 15:54, 55 KJV).

This note of victory is possible not only because Christ has given us eternal life, but also because He has gone before us and has Himself experienced physical *death*. And because of this, we do not have to experience death alone. Hebrews 2: 9–11 says that Jesus experienced death so that He could indeed call us "brothers." He shares every aspect of our humanity, and even in death can say, "Take My hand, follow Me, you'll be walking where I have walked, I'll be with you."

> Since we, God's children, are human beings—made of flesh and blood—He became flesh and blood too by being born in human form; for only as a human being could He die and in dying break the power of the devil who had the power of death. *Only in that way could he deliver those who through fear of death have been living all their lives as slaves to constant dread.*
> Hebrews 2:14, 15 LB (italics added)

This freedom from enslavement to fear can begin as soon as we begin to accept the fact of our physical death. The wisdom and power of the principle of acceptance is bound up in the words of Jesus: "For whoever wishes to save his life shall lose it; but whoever loses his life for My sake shall find it" (Matthew 16:25 NAS).

The fear of death causes us to clutch desperately at life. This is expressed, ultimately, in our society's confused life-style and point of view that is on the one hand unconsciously aware of death's "deadline," yet on the other would pretend that death doesn't exist. But Jesus has broken the chains of fear and dread and would have us open our "clutching hands," as it were, and give to Him not only our lives, *but also the moment of our death.*

Entrusting the moment of physical death to the Lord is valid and appropriate because of who He is. He is no less than the "eternal Spirit" (Hebrews 9:14 KJV), living beyond the limits of time; the only One capable of being with us and near us *forever.* He is the Almighty God, the Everlasting Father, the Prince of Peace—and we know that anything *He* provides will be good. He is our Father, loving and caring for us as His children; He is our Brother, understanding all our feelings; He is the omnipotent God, who alone is capable of changing our feelings, our fears, and our total outlook on both life *and* death.

In the very act of entrusting our death (with our related fears) to the Lord, *we accept its inevitability*—something each one of us must do. And it helps, too, if we accept the fact not only within our hearts, but also verbally—that is, aloud, to others. We need not only to "believe in our hearts" that God will richly care and provide for us at the time of death, but that belief must be brought to reality and "certified" by openly confessing this newly realized fact with our voices. The importance of this verbal breakthrough is apparent when we recall the most obvious manifestation of the fear of death—the absolute unwillingness to talk about it.

This conscious acceptance wrought by the Holy Spirit can bring liberation. Indeed, it is *only* after we allow the Lord to liberate us from the fear of death that we can be free in communicating faith, hope, and comfort to others in their time of confrontation with death. And so yet again we come back to the eternal wisdom and power of what Jesus said: "For whoever wishes to save his life shall lose it; but whoever loses his life for My sake shall find it" (Matthew 16:25 NAS).

David Ray paraphrases the truth of this verse when he says, "Only when you are willing to let go with human life are you really equipped to hold on to life and meaningfully enjoy it."[7] So not only does the entrustment of our physical death into God's hands bring freedom from fear, but it also has a generative power which is bound up in the phrase from Matthew, ". . . shall find it [life]."

> It is the denial of death that is partially responsible for people living empty, purposeless lives; for when you live as if you'll live forever, it becomes too easy to postpone the things you know that you must do. . . . In contrast when you fully understand that each day you awaken could be the last one you have, you take the time *that day* to grow, to become more of who you really are, to reach out to other human beings.[8]

It is only then, as we accept the matter of the quantity of our life, that we can truly appreciate its quality. Accepting the quantity of life tends to prompt a profound reexamination of our life which can stimulate constructive and desirable change. At the same time, instead of our intellectual and emotional energies being siphoned off by the fear of death, we are able now to invest our energies in plans and activities that will enrich our lives, and the lives of those around us. Before, life's limitation—death—was the ruler, the victor. Now death becomes your servant, urging you forward to a more joyous, fruitful, productive life.

Accepting the Fact of Eternal Life

Even though physical death has been accepted, together with the assurance of God's presence and provision in death, most human beings have the deep awareness that life was intended to have a significance beyond its "threescore and twenty years." There is something within most of us that says life must have an eternal dimension. It is as though God had especially placed that truth in the heart of man. And the good news is that it's true—God *has* created life to be everlasting!

This yearning finds its true satisfaction when we understand and accept as our own the Gospel of Jesus Christ. Jesus said, "I am the resurrection, and the life; he that believeth on me, though he die, yet shall he live; and whosoever liveth and believeth on me shall never die. Believest thou this?" (John 11:25, 26 ASV).

That question is directed toward each one of us. For it is all too easy for the Christian to begin to assent to only an *intellectual* belief about eternal life, while the emotions are slowly seduced into that fear-mentality that is so much a part of the world around us. But *the fact of the Resurrection, with its meaning for all mankind, is the great hope of the Christian faith.* And it should be a primary source of strength and energy and joy to every Christian.

One of the most succinct summations of Resurrection faith that I have ever come across was written by Dan Thrapp in the *Los Angeles Times* a few years ago:

Someone has said that the Christian—or his church—"believes" there is life after death, but cannot "know" it because no one can know what lies beyond death. The Easter
story negates that view. By His return, Jesus answered viv-
idly, by His own experience, that there is life after death,
and that it is good. That it is a life of awareness. The difficulty arises when men attempt to interpret their faith in
terms of rational quality or intellect. Intellect tells them
that, once an individual is dead, he remains so. Faith—and
Scripture—tell him that this is not true.

What reason do we have for believing the Resurrection
aside from pure faith? Well, the record, for one thing. Evidence. A band of scattered, demoralized disciples, none
apparently particularly sensitive or psychologically aware,
abruptly became convinced, devoted founders of a world-
wide faith, each of them revealing courage unto death,
often an agonizing death by torture, for the total conviction
that suddenly had overwhelmed them. No interpretation
of the Resurrection as a misty, psychological dream or vision or opinion could account for that stupendous event.
But the fact could. The fact of the Resurrection. The fact
that was recorded by simple, earthy men in the New Testament, the fact that alone could generate their surge of
faith, the fact that Christians have believed ever since.[9]

So our faith in life after death is based on historical fact, and
Christ's personal promise to each of us. Jesus said, "After a little
while the world will behold Me no more; but you will behold
Me; because I live, you shall live also" (John 14:19 NAS).

It is a faith that does not violate reason. In fact, as David Ray
says, it ". . . gives reason something which it desperately needs
—hope! From such hope, reason can claim death as a good and
victorious encounter between the manifestation of life in two
spheres; natural (here) and supernatural (beyond here)."[10]

The Ultimate "Passage"

For the Christian, death is a passage between two qualities
of eternal life. Because of receiving Jesus, "the Eternal Spirit,"
into our lives, our everlasting life begins the very moment we
receive Christ by faith.

> And the witness is this that God has given us eternal life and this life is in His Son. He who has the Son has the life.
>
> 1 John 5:11, 12 NAS

Our life on earth is a pilgrimage during which we progressively learn and experience more and more about that spiritual, heavenly citizenship which is eternal. And it is our privilege to taste of that "eternal" quality of life while on earth. Baron F. Von Hugel wrote: "Only an eternal life already begun and truly known in part here, though fully to be achieved and completely to be understood hereafter, corresponds to the deepest longings of man's spirit as touched by the prevenient Spirit, God."[11] It is the passage of death that allows us to cast off the limitations of our flesh, our "earthboundness," and to fully experience an undiluted everlasting life in the presence of Christ.

> For our earthly bodies, the ones we have now that can die, must be transformed into heavenly bodies that cannot perish but will live forever. When this happens, then at last this Scripture will come true—"Death is swallowed up in victory."
>
> 1 Corinthians 15:53-55 LB

So "Death is not a limit, but a process through which change is made."[12]

All Things Work Together for Good—All Things!

More often than not, Jesus described His death as glorification: "The hour has come for the Son of Man to be glorified" (John 12:23 NAS). ". . . Jesus spoke of dying as a time of exaltation—not a tragedy, a perversion of justice, an accident, a colossal blunder in the divine planning, and a withdrawal of God's love."[13]

A while back, I was discussing with a friend of mine the things he learned while going through the prolonged illness and eventual death of his wife. For months, his wife refused to accept the fact of her dying. Then, about a year before her death, in a small-group Bible study, the Spirit of God mercifully opened her mind and heart to the reality of eternal life

—not as a doctrine of the church, but as her own personal possession at a time of great need. The experience brought new meaning and joy to both of their lives, and helped them both to face her death a year later.

Reflecting on what he learned, my friend said this: "As a Christian you've got a perspective on eternity. Life is no longer 'that big' or an issue of 'how much of it is left.' Life is all a preparation for something else and it is all going to be useful. It doesn't end. So you get a whole different view of where you're going. Every second becomes priceless."

If the seconds are priceless, *what about the years?* Specifically, what about the years in the second half of your life?

I invite *you* to discover a priceless treasure—a life liberated from the fear of death! It will take courage. It will mean facing reality. *But you can do it!*

Accept the fact of physical death, and give that moment into the arms of your heavenly Father. Then, begin to walk in the sunshine of conscious acceptance of eternal life!

Source Notes

1. Quoted in Peter Chew, *The Inner World of the Middle-Aged Man* (New York: Macmillan Co., 1976), p. 6.
2. Quoted in Elisabeth Kübler-Ross, *Death: The Final Stage of Growth* (Englewood Cliffs, N.J.: Prentice-Hall, Inc., 1975), p. 5.
3. Kübler-Ross, op. cit., p. 28.
4. Herb Barks, *Prime Time—Moving into Middle-Age with Style* (Nashville, Tenn.: Thomas Nelson, Inc., 1978), p. 114.
5. G. Zilboorg, "Fear of Death," *Psychoanalytic Quarterly,* 1943, 12:465–75.
6. Paul Tournier, *Learn to Grow Old* (New York: Harper and Row Publishers Inc., 1972), p. 216.
7. David Ray, *The Forty Plus Handbook* (Waco, Tex.: Word, Inc., 1979), p. 140.
8. Kübler-Ross, op. cit., p. 164.
9. Dan Thrapp, "Easter's Story," *Los Angeles Times,* April 2, 1972, p. 12–A.
10. Ray, op. cit., p. 133.
11. Baron F. Von Hugel, in *Concise Dictionary of Religious Quota-*

tions, William Neil, ed. (Grand Rapids, Mich.: Wm. B. Eerdmans Publishing Company, 1974), p. 112.

12. Barks, op. cit., p. 116.
13. Ray, op. cit., p. 144.

6

Now the Fun Begins

*Everyone has the will to win . . . but fewer people
have the will to prepare to win.*

This is where the fun begins . . . or at least, *can* begin.

Getting specific about planning the second half of your life
can be exciting business, *if* you're willing to expend a bit of
effort—an *enjoyable* effort, I might add. However, it is one
thing to think "philosophically" about your future; it is quite
another to begin to take those practical steps that will build
that future! To repeat, *everyone* has the will to win; but fewer
people have the will to *prepare* to win! And that's where the
rubber hits the road.

> Philosophy is important; attitudes make a world of differ-
> ence. But without responsible planning, positive attitudes
> and cheerful philosophies are crushed by the hard facts of
> . . . need.[1]

This applies as much to the Christian as anyone else—in fact,
even more so, because all that we have and hold is God's, and
we are meant to live as stewards of *His* resources. Again, we've
all heard people say: "Don't plan ahead. Just trust the Lord and
He will provide." Few of these people live well in retirement,
however, because that general attitude spills over into their
work and saving habits, preventing them from diligently setting and meeting goals. Remember the passage in Proverbs:
"Go to the ant, thou sluggard; consider her ways, and be wise:
Which having no guide, overseer, or ruler, provideth her meat
in the summer, and gathereth her food in the harvest" (6:6–8
KJV).

For certain, our plans and goals should be laid at the feet of
the Lord of life, subject to the guidance and authority of His
Word. And they should be born out of prayer and counsel with
others. *But they should be made.* The setting of goals is a
healthy exercise and highly motivational:

Holy goals, established in our hearts by God Himself, faithfully prayed over, joyfully desired and received, will lead us into new and wonderfully disciplined lives.[2]

But What Do I Plan *For*?

Plans and goals cannot be created in a vacuum. We first have to know what to plan for. We need to know the areas of primary concern in preparing for our retirement years, which—let me remind you—could be anywhere from one fourth to one third of our life span. And never forget that we don't just retire *from* something; we need also to retire *to* something!

Fortunately, the road of retirement preparation has been well traveled. We can learn much from both the mistakes and successes of those who have taken it before us.

The following chapters discuss four subjects of primary importance in preparing for your retirement years: money, work, health, and relationships.

I invite you to draw upon each chapter as the raw material from which you can fashion the dreams and plans for what can be the most fulfilling portion of your life. And remember, you're not alone in this venture: you're in partnership with the One about whom it was said: ". . . Everything He does is wonderful . . ." (Mark 7:37 LB).

A man's mind plans his way, but the Lord directs his steps and makes them sure.
Proverbs 16:9 AMPLIFIED

He helps me do what honors him the most.
Psalms 23:3 LB

Where is the man who fears the Lord? God will teach him how to choose the best.
Psalms 25:12 LB

Source Notes

1. Maggie Mason, "Creative Retirement," *Christian Life,* May 1979.
2. Charlotte Hale Allen, *Full-Time Living* (Old Tappan, N.J.: Fleming H. Revell Company, 1978), p. 88.

7

Money Is *Important*

Earn all you can; save all you can; give all you can.

JOHN WESLEY

True, there are a lot of things in this world more important than money. But consider these facts:

Item: A Harris poll showed that the number-one reason people feel unfulfilled in retirement is financial problems.[1] *Item:* "Nearly half of retired persons depend on subsistence-level Social Security benefits and a minor amount from pensions as their biggest source of income . . . ."[2] *Item:* Dr. Robert N. Butler reports that "over half of our elderly population live in deprivation."

> I am not speaking of lacking money enough to visit one's grandchildren, keep chilled drinks in the refrigerator, or buy a subscription to the local newspaper. I mean lacking food, essential drugs, a telephone to call for help in emergencies.[3]

No, money isn't everything, but it happens to be close to indispensable if we're to have food, shelter, clothing, and a measure of health and security during life's second half. Dr. Paul Tournier reminds us:

> Life changes entirely if a retired person enjoys a certain measure of financial ease, even a modest one, instead of having to count every penny and to go without everything except what is required merely to subsist.[4]

When You Think Future—Think Inflation

As we begin to think about planning for our future financial security, it is important to realize exactly what we are dealing with. Most important, the value of today's dollar can simply not be used to project future retirement income. Even as we plan, we are faced with the compounding multiplication of costs as we move toward those retirement years. We must therefore understand both the symptoms and effects of our generation's peculiar plague: inflation.

Even though inflation has become a household word, many of us fail to connect its implications with *our* futures:

> Employees typically are not informed about the impact that inflation will have on the purchasing power of their private pensions. A pension that seems adequate at the time of retirement may become inadequate as time passes, requiring an ever-increasing downward adjustment in living levels as one grows older. The severity of the impact of inflation is not fully realized until many options for generating supplemental retirement income no longer exist.[5]

Take a couple beginning retirement with an annual budget of $10,000. At seven percent inflation, the couple needs $10,700 the next year *just to stay even.* And at the end of a decade, it takes *$19,672* to match the buying power of that first-year income of $10,000! Or look at it another way. The chart that follows shows you that, with seven percent inflation, the projected buying power of $10,000 today will be only $5,083 in ten years, and only $2,584 in 20 years.

And bear in mind that these examples are based upon a seven percent inflation rate. At the time this book was written (1980), the inflation rate was at 18 percent, with the most optimistic forecasters projecting an annual rate of 10 percent by year-end. These facts should convince us that our financial planning must take into account the reality of double-digit inflation.

The "Rule of Thumb"

The factor of inflation has drastically changed the experts' "rule-of-thumb" projections of how much income you will need in retirement. Many used to say that, because of decreased expenses during retirement, you need only about half as much money as you earned at the peak of your employment years. (We don't hear too much from those "experts" these days.)

However, even recognizing inflation, many experts still emphasize how much less you'll need in retirement. The problem is that when they say this they are counting on your leading much *less* of a life! Most proposed retirement budgets leave out provisions for vacations, new clothes from time to time, an occasional game of golf, veterinary care for pets, or the simple pleasure drawn from dining out once in a while.

Reprinted from "U.S. News & World Report."

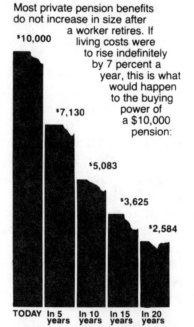

When Inflation Erodes Pensions—

Most private pension benefits do not increase in size after a worker retires. If living costs were to rise indefinitely by 7 percent a year, this is what would happen to the buying power of a $10,000 pension:

$10,000 — TODAY
$7,130 — In 5 years
$5,083 — In 10 years
$3,625 — In 15 years
$2,584 — In 20 years

In short: The pension would buy only one fourth as many goods and services as it would in 1979. Social Security benefits, however, automatically increase as the cost of living goes up.   Source *USN&WR* Economic Unit

Copyright 1979 U.S. News & World Report, Inc.

In our present inflationary economy, one probably needs closer to 60 or 70 percent of his working years' income to be comfortable, perhaps 80 or 90 percent to be well off.[6]

U.S. News & World Report suggests "a retirement income that is nearly 80 percent of working income—not the 60 percent guideline often mentioned in the past."[7]

Let's Start With the Present

The $64,000 question, then, is: "How can I make sure that I'll have that much income during my retirement years?" Well, that's exactly what the remainder of this chapter is about.

One of the very first steps toward answering that question is to fully understand your present financial position. You can't plan for the future until you know all about the present. This involves listing your resources—what you own—and subtracting what you owe, to come up with your net worth. Once you know this, you can both more effectively manage your assets and begin making some decisions for the future.

	Assets (What We Own) John and Mary Smith	Your Figures
Cash:		
Checking account	$ 613	_____
Savings account	3,500	_____
Investments:		
U.S. savings bonds (current cash-in value)	4,000	_____
Stocks, mutual funds	2,500	_____
Life Insurance:		
Cash value, accumulated dividends	5,600	_____
Company Pension Rights:		
(Present annuity value)	20,000	_____
Property:		
House (resale value)	60,000	_____
Furnishings & equipment	10,000	_____
Automobile (resale value)	3,500	_____
Other:		
Loan to friend, no interest	1,000	_____
Gross Assets	$110,713	_____

Liabilities (What We Owe)

Current unpaid bills	$ 570	_____
Home mortgage (remaining balance)	25,000	_____

Auto loan	1,100	————————
Property taxes due	840	————————
Home improvement loan	5,700	————————
Total Liabilities	$33,210	————————

Net Worth: Assets of $110,713 minus
    Liabilities of $33,210 equals $77,503   ————————

The chart above shows how the Smiths figured their net worth. As you continue with this chapter, you will see that some of the Smiths' assets are "lazy," and therefore can't be expected to provide much protection against inflation. For example, their car and household goods are fast losing value. The United States savings bonds and savings-account fund offer a small "cushion" against emergencies, but at present rates of interest neither will grow fast enough to make much of a contribution to an adequate retirement nest egg.

No, the Smiths clearly need to look for ways to be more consistent in their savings. In addition, they need to shift some of those "lazy" assets to more profitable surroundings. They might consider, for example, borrowing from the cash value of their life insurance policy or making a second trust deed loan on the equity of their home, and placing those funds in investments that yield a higher profit during the crucial preretirement years.

The important point is: before anyone can do anything about planning for the future, he needs a clear "fix" on his *present* financial position. Action for Independent Maturity (AIM) gives these tips on figuring net worth:

1. Be honest with yourself. Your assets are worth what you can *sell* them for—*not* what you paid for them.
2. Stocks and bonds should be valued at the present market price.
3. Your pension rights (if vested) and/or your share in a company's profit-sharing plan are a part of your net worth.
4. Don't forget to consider the cash value of your insurance policies.
5. Your home or other real property is worth no more than it would bring on the market (minus sales commissions).
6. In general, household goods are worth far less than you paid for them new or what they would cost to replace.
7. You can make your net-worth statement as simple or as

detailed as you wish. However, it should be complete enough to show how you stand *now* in order to measure your financial progress in the future.[8]

Where Will the Money Come From?

Now that you've determined your net worth (and have a fairly good handle on your present financial position), you can begin to look at the potential sources of *future* income. First, we'll take a look at some of the more common sources. Areas like Social Security, pensions, and life insurance tend to be a bit more humdrum than stocks and real estate, but "Hang in there," because it's *all* important—and also, you have to make sure the first bases are covered before moving on to the more "exotic" subjects.

Social Security

Social Security benefits provide the income foundation for most retirees in the United States.

> Nearly 22 million workers and their dependents plus another 7.5 million survivors of workers, get monthly retirement benefits. The problem is that many people expect too much of Social Security.[9]

Betty Sims, retirement-plans administrator for the Delaware Management Company, goes on to say that Social Security "was never meant to make us independent, only to prevent mass destitution."[10] At 65, a retired worker can expect right now to receive a maximum of $572 a month. A spouse's full benefits amount to half that much, for a combined maximum of $858 per month. (One advantage for retirees is that Social Security payments do climb as inflation does.)

The tragedy is that, even though Social Security was intended "only to prevent mass destitution," the Senate Committee on Aging reports that "the majority of retirees rely on Social Security as the *major or only source of retirement income.*"[11]

Although Social Security payments are far from adequate by themselves, they will be a valuable supplement to your other retirement income. For planning purposes, at any rate, it is important for you to know if you are now qualifying for Social Security benefits, and if your earnings are being correctly credited to your account. To obtain a statement of the amount of earnings credited to your Social Security fund, ask your nearest Social Security Administration office for postcard Form OAR-7004.

Your Company Pension or Profit-Sharing Plan

If you are now a part of either a private or company pension plan, it is most important that you understand the plan thoroughly, and can accurately estimate what your benefits will be.

Because pensions vary so widely, experts advise workers to look for the answers to the questions below, either in their pension handbooks, or from their employers directly:

1. What happens to my benefits if I retire before age 65? later than that?
2. Do the benefits that are stated include Social Security payments?
3. How long must I work for the firm before qualifying for any benefits? before I receive full benefits?
4. How will the payments be made—in a lump sum, monthly, or annually?
5. How are the benefits calculated? Is the amount defined, or does it depend on the investment earnings of the company's pension contributions?
6. What happens to my payments in case of my disability, or in case of interruptions in the period I've worked (such as maternity leaves or layoffs)?
7. Are the benefits lost if I die before retirement, or can my widow(er) collect all or part of the benefits?[12]

Do-It-Yourself Pension Plans

If you are employed, but not covered by a company pension or profit-sharing plan, you can set up your own Individual Retirement Account (IRA). Under the terms of these plans, the government allows you to put aside 15 percent of your annual earnings, up to a maximum of $1,500, with that amount being tax-deductible.

In addition, earnings that build up in the account are tax-deferred until the individual begins withdrawing the money at any time between ages 59½ and 70½. By then, the person is likely to be in a lower tax bracket.[13]

The graph below shows very clearly the advantages to this type of methodical saving plan.

Reprinted from "U.S. News & World Report."

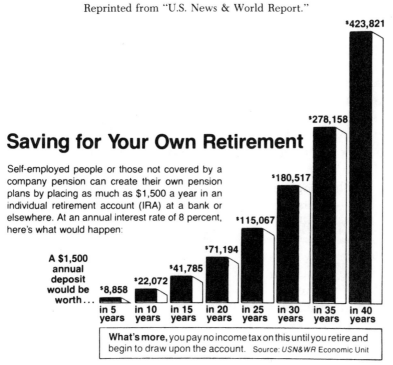

Saving for Your Own Retirement

Self-employed people or those not covered by a company pension can create their own pension plans by placing as much as $1,500 a year in an individual retirement account (IRA) at a bank or elsewhere. At an annual interest rate of 8 percent, here's what would happen:

A $1,500 annual deposit would be worth...

	in 5 years	in 10 years	in 15 years	in 20 years	in 25 years	in 30 years	in 35 years	in 40 years
	$8,858	$22,072	$41,785	$71,194	$115,067	$180,517	$278,158	$423,821

What's more, you pay no income tax on this until you retire and begin to draw upon the account. Source: *USN&WR* Economic Unit

If you are self-employed, you can take advantage of a similar plan, called the Keogh Plan. Under this arrangement, you can put aside 15 percent of your income each year up to $7,500— again, with no tax obligation until you retire. Banks, savings and loan associations, insurance companies, mutual funds, and stockbrokers all offer Keogh plans.

With either of these plans, it is important that you consistently invest 10 percent to 15 percent of your earnings each working year. Your payments into your retirement plan will therefore increase proportionately with your income. In that way, during your working years, your investing will keep pace with inflation.

For further information about both IRA and Keogh plans, ask at the bank or savings and loan association where you do business.

Savings Plans and Liquidity

One of the first things that every financial expert advises for sound financial planning is a ready cash reserve set aside for emergencies. Again, there are numerous rules of thumb for figuring the amount. However, most financial advisers seem to agree that something between three to six months' after-taxes take-home pay should be set aside in a savings account. People more active and experienced in investments tend to keep this liquid reserve at a minimum, since it yields comparatively little income in a savings account. However, only after you feel that you have a sufficient reserve for emergencies, is it wise to move into higher-yield investments.

The Hare and the Tortoise—You Need Both

Before we go any further, I want to urge you again to consider the value of consistent saving.

When you're in your 30s and early 40s, savings plans can seem like a rather slow, somehow "old-fashioned" form of investment. Because of this, it is easy to bypass such plans and move on to other types of investment that can yield *more— faster.* It is true that other investments will bring a higher yield, and it is also true that, in your younger years, you can usually afford to take more and greater risks. However, the key to any sound investment program is *diversity.* No one should put all his eggs in one basket—especially if it's a risky basket! Furthermore, the savings account is an opportunity to let the years ahead of you work for you.

The chart below shows you what a small investment of $50 each month can add up to at a return of just 4½, 5, and 6 percent.

Earning Money Through Savings

How $50 invested each month and compounded semiannually will grow.

Year	4½%	5%	6%
1	$ 614.50	$ 616.50	$ 619.50
2	1,257.50	1,264.00	1,277.00
3	1,929.50	1,944.00	1,974.50
4	2,632.00	2,659.00	2,714.50
5	3,336.50	3,410.00	3,499.50
6	4,134.50	4,199.00	4,332.00
7	4,937.00	5,028.00	5,215.50
8	5,776.50	5,899.00	6,152.00
9	6,654.50	6,814.00	7,147.50
10	7,572.00	7,775.00	8,202.00

Action for Independent Maturity

Anyone Can Begin to Save—and Everyone Needs To!

If your income and your assets are quite limited, you may look at subjects like stocks, bonds, annuities, and real estate with despair, concluding that they are clearly out of your reach. But anyone can earn something in a savings account, however modest.

Let me plead with you not to be discouraged by limited resources. Commit what you have to the Lord. Ask Him to help you learn how to manage the money that you have—and to show you where you could start saving, and preparing for your retirement. Following is a "for instance" of what can happen with just a few dollars.

Suppose that you are nearing retirement, and from a small income you manage to put $100 a month in a savings account that pays you 5½ percent interest, compounded daily. In five years, your money (including interest) would total $6,876. If you chose to take that $6,876 and invest it in a certificate of deposit for six years or more—at a savings and loan institution at seven percent, let us say—it would pay you annual interest of $554, with the principal remaining intact!

So you need both the hare and the tortoise working for you. And don't dismiss the tortoise: he takes patience and perseverance, true, but he'll come through for you if and when you need him.

Life Insurance

The next building block in constructing your future financial security is life insurance. As you probably know, there are two types of life-insurance coverage: "term" life insurance, and "whole" (or "straight") life insurance.

Term insurance provides money for your survivors if you die during the *term* of the policy (which is usually five, ten, or twenty years). You can renew the policy at the end of each term, although your premiums increase as you grow older. On the average, term-insurance premiums cost about half as much as premiums for whole life. Therefore, for young people especially, term insurance is a good way of getting basic protection at relatively low cost.

Whole—or straight—life insurance protects your family in case of your death, while at the same time allowing you to accumulate savings. Unlike term insurance, whole life never expires and the premiums remain the same throughout your life.

If you keep your whole-life policy until you die (at which time your beneficiary family collects the insurance), the underlying savings plan—or "cash value" of the policy—becomes irrelevant. However, if you wish to cash in your policy during your lifetime to take advantage of your accumulated savings, the insurance protection is cancelled. You can also borrow at a low rate of interest—usually five to six percent a year— against the cash value of your policy. This is an excellent "emergency fund" from which you can borrow when you have to.

Some financial advisers suggest that, rather than letting your cash value lie idle (a "lazy" asset), yielding a very low rate of interest, you should borrow on that cash value (at five or six percent interest) and put that money to work in investments that will yield a higher return. Though this is a valid option, it demands careful consideration, because all borrowed money not paid back into your cash-value fund is deducted from the face value of the policy at the time of redemption.

Some experts recommend that you should have insurance equal to five times your annual salary. But the amount varies widely, depending on your family's needs. Once you have established your emergency reserve and have satisfied yourself that your insurance coverage is adequate, you are ready to try to make your nest egg grow.[14]

A Man's Home Is His Castle—*and* His Best Investment

Quite possibly the best investment you will ever make is the purchase of your home. Few types of investment have risen comparably in value in recent years: 13.5 percent in 1978 and 18.9 percent in 1979, for example. Typically, a house bought in 1969 for $21,300 was worth $57,900 in 1979—and even more in certain prime areas.[15] If your house is in a good neighborhood in a good area, its value will more than likely continue to rise. That's more than can be said for any other kind of property—and you get to use and enjoy it at the same time!

In addition, when you own your own home you receive income-tax deductions for the interest on the mortgage and property taxes; and, when you sell, you can receive credits for improvements:

> Under special situations, there are no taxes on part or all of the profits of a sale: (1) when within 18 months before or after the sale, you purchase or start construction of another principal residence; (2) when the house is sold in connection with a new work location such as a company-forced move. In addition, there is a one-shot $100,000 exemption on gains when the owner is 55 or over and has lived in the house three of the last five years.[16]

The dramatic increase in real-estate values during the past five years has substantially raised the equity of many people's homes (another "lazy" asset). This has prompted many people either to refinance their homes, or to take second trust deed loans and use these funds for investment purposes.

Four years ago, a 36-year-old friend, Larry Benton, did just that. He and his wife refinanced their home, and used a portion of the cash to remodel their kitchen. With the remainder of the funds, they purchased a one-tenth share in one apartment and a one-sixth share in another. The initial total outlay for both investments was $8,000. Four years later, one investment had yielded $8,000 profit and the other $23,000 profit. Those funds have now been placed into other investments, including real estate and stocks.

Larry and his wife were fortunate, because most investments don't yield that much so quickly. But the point is that, as the Bentons' investment portfolio grows, I'm sure they will always point back to a beginning—and that was the day they bought a house.

And Now Those Stocks

Corporate stocks and bonds are often the heart of investment programs. When you buy a share of *common stock,* you are buying a share of ownership in a company. From the shares you purchase, you can make money in two ways—from cash dividends that the company pays to stockholders, and through the rise in the value of the stock itself.

A sound perspective on common stocks is given by C. Colburn Hardy in his book *Your Money and Your Life:*

> Over the long term of financial planning, the rewards of quality common stocks can be substantial, but such stocks are not *always* the best investments. Far from it. They must be managed: sold when they become overpriced, when total returns do not meet your financial needs, or when there is a decline in the market and/or stock value. That is the time to put the proceeds in fixed-income holdings and wait until the economic outlook is brighter and stock market values are rising. Quality common stocks should be the core of any long-term financial planning investment program, but just as with all your assets, they should be sold and bought to achieve the greatest total returns.[17]

When you buy a *corporate bond* or a *government bond,* you are lending a corporation or a municipality money for which you are *regularly* paid a fixed rate of interest. Bonds are issued for a specific period of time—ten to twenty years or more. When they mature, you get back the face amount of the bond.

High-quality corporate bonds are usually a safe investment; however, they have their disadvantages. They usually must be bought in large denominations—$1,000 is usually the minimum—and they can fluctuate widely on the open market, in response to the ups and downs in interest rates. So if prices decline, you may have to wait until the maturity date to get back the face amount of the bond.

No two people approach investment in stocks and bonds in exactly the same way, but investment counselors say that, as a general rule, the younger a person—or the more assets he holds—the greater risk he can afford to take. As a person nears retirement, however, the strategy should focus on producing and protecting income. (People in their 30s and 40s might focus on growth-type stocks and mutual funds.)

> The younger person, for example, might sink 80 percent of his investment capital into stocks and only 20 percent into bonds. For people age 45 to 55, the balance would tip to 60–40. Then for those whose retirement is near, the emphasis would shift to steady income . . . perhaps 80 percent of a portfolio for an older worker might be in bonds and 20 percent in high-grade stocks.[18]

Again, AIM gives us some good principles for stock investment:

> 1. Define your objectives and invest with a purpose. Do you want maximum growth of your principal, or do you want a high yield dividend?
> 2. Your objectives should be tailored to your present and future needs. (This would depend upon your age and how far or near you are to retirement.)
> 3. You should plan your stock investments as *part* of your total program, and not put all of your nest egg in one basket.
> 4. In buying a company's stock, you actually are acquiring part ownership of the business. Find out about the company. Any broker will supply you with background information on many stocks.
> 5. Handle your stock investments through established, reliable securities firms. Don't buy wildcat stocks from fast-

talking salesmen, and don't be pushed into buying any security hurriedly on the basis of irresponsible "tips."[19]

An Answer to "What Securities Should I Buy?"

Mutual funds are one answer to that perplexing question. A mutual fund is a group investment plan in which an investor combines his money with that of hundreds of other investors. These funds are then invested in a broad spectrum of securities of various types: common stocks (both speculative and conservative); preferred stocks; corporate bonds; and—perhaps—government bonds. As an individual investor, you do not own all or part of any of these securities as such. Rather, you own a share in the mutual-fund company's total portfolio.

Many types of mutual funds have been formed to meet the varying needs of investors: growth funds, long-term growth-of-capital funds, income funds, balanced funds, and more.

As with common stocks, shares in mutual funds can go down as well as up in value. Some have been mismanaged, so a choice of a mutual fund demands careful study. It is important to check past performance during both up and down periods in the stock market.

> Two other useful clues are the length of time a fund has been in operation and the amount of its total assets. A small fund may be unable to achieve a good "mix" of assets and too large a fund may be inflexible. Some mutual-fund consultants suggest that $50 million to $250 million in total assets is a good range.[20]

Annuities Pay *You*

In purchasing an annuity from an insurance company, a Christian investors organization, or other source, you are actually exchanging money for the organization's promise to pay you an agreed-upon amount periodically, beginning at a designated age and continuing until death. There are many types of annuities, including those which will pay benefits to your spouse after your death.

Annuities draw interest during your working years, but you

pay no income tax on that interest until you collect it—when your tax bracket may well be lower. The principal advantages of an annuity are that you know the *exact* income it will provide after retirement, and you have the security that you will never outlive that particular income. On the other hand, annuities usually do not yield a high rate of interest, so they are a poor hedge against inflation. Their purpose is not as a "growth" investment, but as a steady source of certain income during retirement years.

One Way It Can Work

Let me give you a personal illustration of what can happen through a stock investment linked with an annuity program. Ten years ago, I bought $5,000 worth of stock in a book-and-record–publishing company. Seven years later, the company was bought out by a conglomerate, and my stock was then worth $12,000. It continued to climb in value until it was worth $44,000. At that point, my wife and I decided we wanted to give that money to the ministry of World Vision in the form of a unitrust annuity. In doing so, we received a sizable tax break on the stock profits we had earned and we are now receiving a quarterly check from the trust. We have the pleasure of knowing that our funds are being used in worldwide ministry, while receiving a yearly income of close to $3,500—an amount equal to a full 70 percent of my original investment!

I made that original purchase of stock at 50 years of age. So be encouraged, friend—no matter where you are in life, no matter what your age, you can start to think, and to plan. There are ways to not only make your assets grow, but ways to legally and ethically reduce your tax obligation while providing yourself with a steady income. And annuities are one such way.

Annuities and trusts can be set up with many Christian nonprofit organizations. Investigate the possibilities with your tax accountant, lawyer, or an officer of the nonprofit institution. The development departments of some denominations and Christian organizations often have full-time personnel available to help in estate planning in which annuity trusts are a vital part.

Income Property—What the Stories Are All About

Income property (or "improved" property), such as houses, apartment buildings, and commercial structures, can be one of the most rewarding of all investments. Not only are there profits to be derived from the appreciation of the property, but you can receive tax benefits from the depreciation of the building on it. However, if a person buys "on a shoestring," maintenance costs and today's rising taxes can become a bottomless pit that consumes not only profits but also funds borrowed to survive in the event of vacancies or other negative circumstances.

In *How to Avoid the Retirement Trap,* Leland Cooley points out some necessary temperament traits for this type of investment:

> This sort of investment can work miracles for those who understand the principle involved and who have the innate ability and enthusiasm to begin modestly and pyramid their holdings through a process of *buy cheap, fix up, sell at a profit and start the whole process over again on a larger scale.* [21]

Because of the demands of apartment (or other structure) management and maintenance, this investor must be willing and able to confront both people and problems, as well as have the ability to pick up hammer, saw, or plumber's wrench to make repairs "on call." (The alternative to this is to have the surplus funds to pay to have necessary work done, which many do—although the cost can be high.)

If you don't have this kind of temperament or ability, there are opportunities to buy shares in limited partnerships of real-estate syndicates. In these arrangements, you own a portion of a building (or buildings) with others, giving authority to a general partner to take care of the management and maintenance of your investment. In return, the general partner receives an extra percentage of profits when the unit(s) are sold.

This can be a worry-free and profitable arrangement, *provided* you can trust the character and experience of the general partner. Legally, the future of your investment is in his hands, dependent on his integrity and competence:

To invest wisely, the investor must have a good sense of property values, be able to appraise future earning potential and resale opportunities, and know the business reputation of the principals who are involved.[22]

Be Cautious—but Don't Be Scared Off Too Soon, Either

In either case—complete ownership or partnership—the potential pitfalls in real-estate investment are often emphasized. And while I would encourage you to consider those potential problems, don't let them discourage you from considering some such investment. Any profitable investment program demands study, energy, and work. If you approach your investment program as something "on the side," with a "strategy" of "trying this and trying that"—it won't work. You need to consider your investment program as "part-time employment," and be willing therefore to work through the problems and expend some effort in order to gain the rewards—because, believe me, the rewards are worth the investment!

Unimproved Land

Although money can be made from this type of investment, it should be approached with caution. So long as land remains undeveloped and produces no income, while still involving some costs (such as taxes), it should be thought of as a long-range and to some some degree speculative investment. Beware especially of recreational property a great distance from your home—particularly, as advertised by a "developer." In most cases, the profits in the land have already been taken by the development company. Projected profits to buyers will depend greatly upon supply and demand, and upon the rate and quality of the development in the area. It is usually only the young investor who can afford to wait the long period needed for growth, and—even then—"community improvements" needed to insure growth and increase the value could mean rising taxes and yet new assessments.

My advice is, yes, money can be made in unimproved land, but the investment will probably be more "long-term" than you anticipate or desire. *Ask questions and seek objective professional help before making any such purchase.*

It Pays to Know About Taxes

There are two basic principles of tax policy for you to keep in mind as you plan your preretirement investment program:

(1) To the extent practical, try to invest in assets that produce capital gain, rather than full taxable income. Investments held for longer than a year become long-term capital-gain investments, and benefit from a more favorable tax treatment (rather than being taxed right along with your income).

(2) To the extent practical, postpone taking taxable income from your assets until retirement, when you can expect to be in a substantially lower tax bracket. (This principle would not apply as strongly to the younger investor, of course.)

Income-producing real estate offers special advantages in this area. In addition to the tax-deductible interest on mortgages, real estate taxes and certain other expenses are deductible for income tax purposes. In addition, the value of buildings *(though not of land)* can be depreciated over a period of years, which significantly lowers the capital-gains taxes that must ultimately be paid.

Because few of us fully understand the complexities of the tax system, it is important that you seek the advice of an investment or tax counselor as you develop your investment program. Regular counsel with him can save you taxes and thus income.

Your Investment Strategy

Regardless of the particular abilities or temperament of the investor, most investment counselors recommend what might be called a "self-correcting investment program." With this plan, half of the available investment dollars are placed in savings accounts, certificates of deposit, corporate and municipal bonds, or annuities—that is, in fixed dollars. The other half are placed in common stocks, variable annuities, mutual funds, or real estate partnerships—that is, in growth dollars. (Again, the important thing is not putting all your eggs in one basket.)

Another important element in your investment strategy is your age. If you're in your peak earning years, with investment money more available, this is the time to build equity. Therefore, you might want to consider real estate, growth

stocks, and mutual funds. If, on the other hand, you're nearing retirement, you may feel you can afford to take only a
few chances, depending on how close you've come to approaching your goal. Instead of trying to build equity, then,
you should probably be more concerned with ways to increase your income.

> For example, a paid-up mutual fund can be turned into
> an annuity paying a fixed income. Low-yield growth stocks
> might be sold and converted into Series H savings bonds,
> paying a guaranteed interest rate.[23]

One thing to remember always . . . the old adage, containing
much truth: "Nothing ventured, nothing gained." Put this on
a card and carry it in your billfold or purse, from age 30 to
about age 50.

Be Sure to Reevaluate

If you're a businessman, you've already learned the wisdom
of constantly evaluating programs and policies to see if they
are effectively meeting predetermined goals. The same is true
with a personal investment program. Savings and investment
programs should be reviewed frequently, and should come up
for a *complete* review at appropriate junctures—for example,
when the family is known to be complete; or when a final
career commitment has been made; or when one family mem-
ber begins (or stops) working; and certainly when retirement
is no closer than 15 years away.

Use Your Will Power

People keep reminding you about it . . . you have every good
intention of taking care of it . . . but somehow it never seems
to get done. Somehow, you never get around to making your
will—and maybe for one of these two reasons: you believe your
assets (or "estate") are not large enough to commit to a will, or
you believe a lawyer's services are too costly.

> Such people often fail to recognize just how large their
> estates are because they forget to include assets payable at

death such as life insurance. And when a person adds up
the true value today of home, furniture, automobile, bank
account, and investments, the total may be surprising.
Make no mistake: the tax collector will include them all!
The fear that a lawyer's charge for preparing a will would
be too much is certainly being pennywise and pound foolish. Sure, preparation of a will can cost a few dollars, but it
may save your family thousands.[24]

The facts are very simple, really. If you die without a will,
the state will make one for you. The state will determine who
gets your property, who will carry out legal procedures in
connection with your estate, how much will be paid in taxes,
who will be responsible for minors, and who will receive the
fee for these services.

With a will, *you* determine the outcome in all of those areas:

The right to make a will is a very powerful right indeed.
Use your will power so that the financial security you've
worked so hard to establish doesn't slip away through a lack
of planning.[25]

Begin to Work at It *Now*

Throughout this chapter I've tried to emphasize that saving
and investing some part of our earnings is something we *all*
need to do, to the degree that we can—no matter how modest
our income. Someone has said, "It's not what you make that
counts. It's the difference between what you make and what
you spend that's important." And that "difference" is the portion to save and invest.

This may mean that you need to learn more about how to
manage your money. (It is surprising how many of us who have
been working for a salary all of our lives have gotten used to
letting our salary control our expenses.)

However, I think I know what you're saying about now: "Do
you realize how difficult it is to save, with the cost of living as
it is? The difference between what *we* make and what we
spend is darn little!"

All I can say is, begin working with that "darn little"—today.
Determine your net worth. Search out those "lazy" assets, and
begin to make even the small amount available work for you.

Once you know your present financial position, either find out yourself how you can start to multiply your current assets or seek professional counsel.

Many people, for example, hesitate to consult life insurance companies for an analysis of their financial situation, because they fear that "all they want to do is sell me more insurance!" They probably will—but going through that analytical process is far better than ending up without adequate income at 65 or 70.

Whatever your age, you need to make sure you are managing your finances, and that they are not managing you.

The Great House With Many Rooms

So often, I believe, we look at our lives as a large house that has many rooms, designated: family, career, relationship with God, finances, friends at work, friends at church, and so forth. Unconsciously, we see ourselves moving from room to room in our house throughout the day, with each activity separate from the others. Very easily, then, "spiritual things" can come to have a room of their own, quite separate and apart from the other rooms—especially, the room called "finances" or "money."

God would have us remove those walls of separation—those barriers between the various "rooms" of our life. He wants *one* room, into which He breathes life; He wants to "condition" the entire atmosphere with His life and presence. He wants to be as much a part of preparing your future financial security as preparing next Sunday's Bible study class.

In their book *The Best Half of Life*, my friends Ray and Anne Ortlund ask the question, "What is money for?" They then answer it as follows:

> So what is money really for?
>
> To glorify God. You must not glory in money itself. Rather, handle your money with the sure knowledge that He personally gave it to you, in the amount He wanted you to have, to handle for Him. . . .
>
> To provide everything you need to live abundantly for Him. The last two words are utterly important: *for Him.*
>
> To see God's power and love in providing for you. . . . If you put God to the test concerning His promises, He can

use physical resources to increase your faith and conquer your worry. . . .

To unite in a wonderful way the family of God. . . . Saying "I love you" to a fellow Christian is a beautiful and important thing to do—but slipping him money when he needs it certainly adds to the ring of authenticity.[26]

The First Shall Be Last

Ray and Anne then add a thought that I've saved to conclude this chapter, because—for the Christian—it is the most important "investment strategy" of all. After you've determined your present financial position, and you are ready to begin planning for the years ahead, begin with this powerful principle:

> First, give. Give the first and the best. Let your gift to God be the first check written every payday, and give until you're a little breathless and dizzy; give through and beyond that pain threshold to the place where, if He doesn't come through you're sunk. Then you'll know the exhilaration of the faith-life—whatever your income base may be.[27]

There is no way you can lose when giving is the keystone of your personal economic policy. There are many principles that the Bible presents as cornerstones of a fulfilling, joy-filled life, but one of the most dynamic is this: "Give, and it will be given to you; good measure, pressed down, shaken together, running over, they will pour into your lap. For whatever measure you deal out to others, it will be dealt to you in return" (Luke 6:38 NAS).

If the motive is selfishness, that verse can result in a shoddy "prosperity teaching" that tarnishes its beauty and truth. If the motive is an openhearted love for God and His people, though, that verse becomes an undisputable reality in every area of life —from our personal relationships to our personal financial planning.

Finally, I could write many pages of personal testimony to God's provision of financial resource in time of need, as well as to His provision of the necessary resources when I needed to begin building for the future!

If God Be for You . . .

Well, then . . . are you ready to make those plans? Fine! Get out your financial records, get a pencil and paper—and begin to see exactly "where you're at." Then—possibly with the help of a professional counselor—begin to plan "where you're going."

As Ray and Anne Ortlund indicated, God will use your finances to express His love and care for you. But He wants you to play a part. He wants to be a partner with you. Therefore, begin to move out in faith and action. Pray . . . study the possibilities . . . work . . . and then, confidently expect God to provide the practical direction you need.

And if God be for you, who or what can be against you?

> Riches can disappear fast . . . so watch your business interests closely. Know the state of your flocks and your herds; then there will be lamb's wool enough for clothing, and goat's milk enough for food for all your household after the hay is harvested, and the new crop appears, and the mountain grasses are gathered in.
>
> Proverbs 27:23–27 LB

Source Notes

1. Quoted in Virginia L. Boyack, "Preparing for Retirement: Crisis or Challenge?" Hearing Before the Sub-committee on Retirement Income and Employment of the Select Committee on Aging, House of Representatives, Ninety-fifth Congress, Second Session (Washington, D.C.: U. S. Government Printing Office, 1978), p. 61.
2. Ibid., p. 195.
3. Tony Lamb and Dave Duffy, *The Retirement Threat* (Los Angeles: J. P. Tarcher, Inc., 1977), p. 16.
4. Dr. Paul Tournier, in *The Encyclopedia of Religious Quotations,* Frank S. Mead, ed. (Old Tappan, N.J.: Fleming H. Revell Company, 1965), p. 270.
5. Robert J. Ahrens, "Retirement, Work, and Lifelong Learning," Hearing Before the Special Committee on Aging, United States Senate, Ninety-fifth Congress, Second Session (Washington, D.C.: U. S. Government Printing Office, 1978), p. 226.

6. Peter Mustric, *The Joy of Growing Older* (Wheaton, Ill.: Tyndale House Publishers, 1979), p. 35.

7. "Will Inflation Tarnish Your Golden Years?" *U. S. News & World Report,* February 26, 1979, p. 55.

8. "AIM's Guide to Financial Security," Action for Independent Maturity, Washington, D. C., 1978.

9. "It's Never Too Early to Plan," *U. S. News & World Report,* February 26, 1979, p. 57.

10. Ibid.

11. William C. Wampler, "Preparing for Retirement: Crisis or Challenge?" Hearing Before the Sub-committee on Retirement Income and Employment of the Select Committee on Aging, House of Representatives, Ninety-fifth Congress, Second Session (Washington, D.C., U. S. Government Printing Office, 1978), p. 2.

12. "AIM's Guide to Financial Security."

13. "It's Never Too Early to Plan," op. cit., p. 57.

14. Lee Butcher, *Retirement Without Fear* (Princeton, N.J.: Dow Jones Books, 1978), pp. 27, 28.

15. Joel Singer, "Forecast for the '80s," *California Real Estate,* January 1980, p. 22.

16. C. Colburn Hardy, *Your Money and Your Life* (New York: AMACOM, 1979), p. 110.

17. Ibid., p. 139.

18. "It's Never Too Early to Plan," op. cit., p. 58.

19. "AIM's Guide to Financial Security."

20. Ibid.

21. Leland F. Cooley and Lee Morrison Cooley, *How to Avoid the Retirement Trap* (Los Angeles: Nash Publishing Corporation, 1972), p. 150.

22. "AIM's Guide to Financial Security."

23. Butcher, op. cit., p. 32.

24. "AIM's Guide to Financial Security."

25. Ibid.

26. Raymond and Anne Ortlund, *The Best Half of Life* (Glendale, Calif.: Regal Books, 1976), p. 105.

27. Ibid., p. 106.

8

Retire to *Something—* *Not* From *Something*

When you've been used to doing things, and they've been taken away from you, it's as if your hands had been cut off.

GEORGE ELIOT

Ah, but when I retire, that'll be the life. No jangling alarm waking me up at dawn, no more worries about production schedules or personnel problems, just relaxing days doing what I want to do, when I want to do it!

Sound good? Well, maybe, but—sad to say—there seems to be another side to the story. The experience of all too many retirees is that the "great retirement dream" seldom turns out like it's supposed to. All too often, "doing what *I* want to do when *I* want to do it" translates into a steady diet of boredom, frustration, and disappointment.

And, to a large degree, that's because the "great retirement dream" is based on two fallacies. One is that, when we retire, our whole world will somehow change, including who we are (and who we've always been). Life will be . . . well, "different," just because we'll be . . . well, "retired."

The second fallacy is that life will be at its best and most fulfilling once we are finally free of all those workaday responsibilities, duties, and interpersonal hassles.

You're Not Retiring From Life—or From Yourself

Most of us have learned by now that life actually "owes" us very little. We *do* owe it to ourselves, however, to prepare for the most fulfilling retirement possible. An important part of that preparation is facing up to the fact that, when we retire, we will continue to be the same person we have always been. And life will continue much as it always has. We won't be suddenly transported into a state of "nirvana"—freed somehow from the responsibility of dealing with life as we've known it for some 60-odd years. We will still want to feel needed, worthwhile, productive. We will still need, too, to feel that we're growing, that we're useful, and that our existence is important.

This is why so many retirees, after spending a few vacation-style months on the golf course, come to miss—if not indeed to long for—the shattering sound of the alarm clock waking them up to the involvement and challenge of the world of work. Putter in hand, they come to the startling realization that, on the day they retired, they walked away from a large part of themselves.

Much of the problem, I think, is rooted in the way we have traditionally viewed retirement in this country. It has been stubbornly seen as a withdrawal from activity and responsibility, as if God intended for us to live our best years without those very involvements that produce precisely the sense of self-worth so necessary to health and "wholeness."

Viktor Frankl said that "a human being cannot live a life without meaning; if the meaning is trivial, the life is trivial; if the meaning is exalted, the life is exalted."[1]

Too often our concept of retirement has been just that—a life of triviality. Former Secretary of Labor Willard Wirtz observed:

> I am not at all sure that we are going the right course by encouraging early retirement . . . . Until we come up with a better theory of what people are supposed to do when they get old, I'm not prepared to encourage retirement at all.[2]

Indeed, the traditional view of retirement is rubbing a lot of people the wrong way these days. Appearing before the Senate Committee on Aging, Robert Benedict said:

> The term "retirement" needs to give way to a more generous understanding of the emergence of alternative life cycles involving new combinations of work, education and

leisure in the broader context of living in the later years. Indeed the term "retirement," as we know it, may be obsolete. I personally would not mourn its passing.[3]

The Alarm Clock *Is* Important

Part of the difficulty of retirement adjustment is bound up in what we're actually saying when we use the word: what we mean by retirement is *retirement from work*. And therein lies the problem, because—for most people—that interpretation represents a powder keg of potential trauma:

> Certainly one way to ascertain the importance of work in a person's life is to observe how men act when they are deprived of it. Strong feelings of insecurity usually occur right after the initial shock, which creates intense anxiety in most people. If an individual finds it increasingly difficult to work, depression of varying degrees may result. A feeling of inadequacy may be a tag-along too, because self-esteem is jarred. Indeed, the loss of the settled framework of a job is enormous.[4]

To the person who has invested 20 or 30 years in a meaningful career—whether it be electrical engineering or teaching or homemaking—that career has become an extension of himself. It has brought a sense of worth and dignity, and has therefore been a major source of building self-esteem.

> Work supplies an answer to some of the deepest and most basic of all human drives: the need to produce something, the need to create something, the need to satisfy curiosity, the need to be useful, the need to be needed.[5]

If work is this important to our emotional well-being, then it certainly ought to be one of the primary considerations in our long-range retirement planning.

Why Not Keep the Alarm Clock Handy?

For millions, work is becoming a viable option *after* retirement age. This can mean either part-time paid work, volunteer work, a full-time "second career," or even continuing in one's former career on some sort of "post-retirement" basis.

> Taken together, an estimated three million persons above age 65 are in paid jobs, and 4.5 million others serve in volunteer posts. An additional four million say that they would like to work if they could find an opening.[6]

A 1979 Louis Harris poll found that the trend toward early retirement may be reversed in the not too distant future.

> More than half of today's employees would prefer to continue working—either full-time or part-time, at the same job or a less demanding job—instead of retiring, and just less than half say they actually plan to continue working and defer retirement.[7]

Jarold Kieffer of the Academy for Educational Development adds that "We're rapidly approaching the time when most workers will automatically enter second careers at retirement, simply to remain active or supplement their pensions."[8]

Labor experts give many reasons for this trend. Among the most important are (1) inflation, which has cut deeply into retirement incomes; (2) the abrupt and distressing changes in life-style brought about by retirement; and (3) the twin facts that people are living longer and fewer younger workers are entering the work force, resulting in an increased demand— and increased opportunities—for older workers.

Incidentally, more and more employers are seeing this as a definite plus. A study reported on by the *Harvard Business Review* showed:

> Older managers were better able to accurately appraise the value of the new information . . . . Older people seem to have achieved superior standing among sales workers as well and to have remained higher performers.[9]

Also:

> The United Bank of Illinois solved a problem of younger work dissatisfaction and high error rates in its check-filing and records department by hiring a three-person unit of

retirees. The older employees paid greater attention to detail and were considered more reliable.[10]

"Phasing In" to Retirement

An increasingly popular way to continue working and still "phase in" to retirement is taking a part-time job—or continuing at the same job with an abbreviated schedule. Surprisingly, the permanent part-time work force of America is now the fastest growing segment of the overall employed in our country. In the past fifteen years, this segment has increased by 40 to 50 percent. The growing list of options includes: job sharing, in which two persons work part-time to carry out one full-time job; "tapering off," in the form of a reduced work week; and leaves, sabbaticals, longer vacations, or special work assignments, all of which allow older workers to serve in community projects at full or reduced pay, while at the same time giving them an opportunity to adjust to a life outside the company environment.

The Important Thing Is Growing

Fortunately, the options and available combinations of work, hobbies, recreation, and ministry involvement are many and can be proportioned to fit your future needs, desires, and abilities. Whatever the combination, though, happy is the person who realizes that retirement is not the cessation of productivity and worth. On the contrary, your retirement can represent a giant step of tremendous growth and progress. The key to making this a reality is your taking steps—right now!—to make sure that, when retirement comes, you are retiring *to* something. Something you feel is more worthwhile, yes. Something you enjoy more, yes. Something more of your own choosing, yes. But, most important, *something* that stretches you, keeps you involved in life . . . and keeps you "growing."

Gearing up for this "growing" dimension of retirement begins now. You can't play "catch-up" later. *Now* is the time to begin thinking about retiring—and retiring *to* something.

You Begin by Broadening Your Interests—Now

We have a great tendency in our Western culture to focus our entire life on one career—that one thing in life that we *do.* We commonly begin training for that "one thing" in high school and college. Then, upon graduation, we venture out into the world of work, perhaps having to make some adjustments or detours, but—eventually—we find our "niche" and begin to build "our career."

The problem with many of us is that we soon develop "tunnel vision," with all our interests and energies focused toward one area of life—our work. And because of the havoc this can cause us in retirement, it's important that we use our middle years to broaden our interests. Now is the time to develop interests, abilities, talents that you've toyed with, but never had the opportunity (or the courage!) to pursue, or take the time to cultivate. In his book *How to Stay Younger While Growing Older,* Reuel Howe calls these interests "sustaining enthusiasms" or "passions":

> The passion of love, for instance, is self-forgetting, transforming, and energizing. . . . The maintenance of youthfulness and a desire to grow and live depend in part on pursuing something that really interests us and turns us on. . . . My awareness of these available areas for enthusiastic activity gives me a sense of security for my future. It is great to know that I shall probably never be "unemployed" or lacking in some passionate interest.[11]

Just for Fun . . . and Growth

For certain, one or two or three of these "passions" should be in the category of hobbies or recreation. (It's surprising how many people are so smothered by their work that they don't have time for hobbies!) This should be something you really enjoy doing, "just for fun"—something like gardening, model railroading, making pottery, furniture refinishing, writing, weaving rugs, collecting stamps or coins, rock hunting, traveling, painting, photography, astronomy, epicurean cooking. The list is endless:

> Old pastimes should be re-examined from a fresh point of view. Take reading, for example. Try moving into a brand

new area. If you have always leaned towards novels, try shifting to biographies—and don't stop there. Plunge into a field that has been buzzing around the fringes of your mind for years . . . with the feeling that at long last you will have the time to devote to something that enthuses you, your retirement will loom ahead as a pleasant prospect.[12]

(By the way, it's good to take up at least one hobby as a couple. Learning something together is not only fulfilling *now*, but will reap large dividends upon retirement.)

One area in which to plan early is in the area of sports or physical activity. We'll be dealing with this at greater length in a later chapter, but let me mention now that blessed is the 30- or 40-year-old "jock" who gives up Saturday's horizontal vigil before the tube, watching baseball or football, in favor of learning tennis or golf. He's making an investment not only in his health—physical and emotional—but also in the life he'll be leading 35 years hence.

Just for Fun—and Income!

One of the earliest and most fascinating discoveries of satisfied retirees is that many of the things they were involved in as hobbies become important streams that run together later in life. In addition, many of these "just-for-fun" hobbies can and do become future sources of income. In fact, the best kind of "second career" combines the resources of past experiences with the pure enjoyment and relaxational attributes of a "hobby."

Ted Goodman was an architect before a physical ailment forced him to retire. However, a few years earlier, he had begun to do some planning. While employed, he used much of his spare time getting experience in his hobby, photography. He studied magazines, checked out "how-to" books from the library, and took some adult education courses—not only in photography, but also in picture framing.

By the time retirement came, he had his own equipment and was ready to set up shop. He now has a successful, low-overhead business of his own—one that's fun, doesn't monopolize his time, and provides a good source of income.

Bob Fraid of Napa, California, has spent the last 42 years perfecting the skills of tying fishing flies—a hobby he learned as a lad of 17. Bob is retired from both the U.S. Navy and the state Department of Fish and Game. In learning to tie flies, he has become something of an expert in the study of insects.[13]

Before retiring, Betty Windsor taught college-level history. During her teaching career, she had been on call as a volunteer guide when academic conferences met in her historic university town. For Betty, her town and American history were her "hobby." So, upon retirement, she combined her "hobby" with the experience of her career. She wrote an historical guidebook of her community, let her services as a guide be known, and now she is even more in demand—and this time for pay!

Learn to Love Learning

As *you* search for new areas of interest, don't pass up the many opportunities available for furthering your education. One of the discoveries many mid-lifers make about continuing education is that the fun of "going back to school" can be in the learning itself, as well as in reaping the benefits of increased knowledge (and even additional income) in the years ahead. High schools offer many adult courses at night, including bookkeeping, real estate, interior decorating, dress design, electronics, cabinet making, small-business management, blueprint reading, television repair—you name it!

More Time for a Ministry

Planning early to retire *to* something means that you can plan to do that something "you've always wanted to do." And for the Christian, there is an extra dimension to that dream. Retirement offers a tremendous opportunity to begin that "something" you've always wanted to do "for the Lord."

Sheldon MacDonald has just retired at 66. He spent 17 years in oil refining, then another 22 years in the corporate headquarters of a large oil company. Through the years, he gained broad experience in industrial relations, executive recruitment, planning, development, and budgeting.

One of Shel's after-retirement goals was to be able to offer his experience to churches and Christian organizations at no charge—just as a servant of Jesus Christ. And what a servant heart he has! The MacDonalds are by no means wealthy; however, a part of their financial planning included a real-estate investment, with the goal of paying off their home mortgage by the time they retired.

Today, Shel is involved in financial canvassing for his church, including counseling people in the area of wills and endowments. He is also fundraising for an interdenominational youth organization, as well as offering his expertise in the area of management. He is advising a group of laymen who want to begin organizing and funding a youth outreach in the high schools of their area. And, finally, he's consulting with yet another Christian organization in the area of fundraising and computer accounting.

Shel is now "booked up" three months in advance, and is personally involved in the ministries of at least six organizations—including his own church! He says: "Because of my background, I can help organizations implement their plans and their dreams. Many times, I'm a trouble-shooter; other times, I'm a catalyst to get something moving and off the ground; sometimes, I'm just an encourager."

I should also mention that a few years ago Shel and his wife, Marie, took an intensive, two-year lay-counseling course from a psychologist who attended their church. So they are also "para-counselors," sharing their lives with people who face imminent death, or who have marital problems, or who just need a loving friend during a period of crisis.

Shel and Marie MacDonald are a couple who retired *to* something—and with a plus, because that "something" includes a vital Christian ministry.

You Might As Well Think Big!

Of course, you don't have to stay close to home, either! Many organizations have sprung up in recent years that specialize in placing laymen and lay women in secular employment and/or Christian ministry opportunities overseas. Organizations and industries in Third World countries, for example, need people experienced in food production, engineering and technology, management, finance, health care, and teaching at every level.

Some of the openings are in the short-term missionary service category; others are outright jobs, and provide a moderate income.

Don't say that it couldn't be you! Can you think of anything more exciting than to be able, at 55 or 60 or 65, to retire *to* something that included two, three, or five years in a developing country, learning about another culture, making new friends, while investing your life in a missionary endeavor? Think about it.

As you dream and plan about what you would like to retire *to,* I would suggest that you include two very important ingredients: (1) *involvement* in the lives of other people; and (2) the element of *risk*—risk that forces you to grow.

Involve Yourself With People and the World Around You

As we plan ahead, we need to remember that involving ourselves in the concerns, the problems, the joys, and the day-to-day lives of other people is one of the healthiest and most rewarding things we can do. Such involvement cultivates an outward view of life—and a healthy view. "Others" become a priority; "self" takes a step or two backward.

Personal involvement with others means we are willing to give a part of ourselves (whether that be measured in time or substance), a part of our life, to someone else. Of course, one of the dividends is that such giving comes right back to us in the form of inner joy and vitality. The way to beget life, always, is by giving it away.

However, involvement with others isn't easy. It costs something, in terms of time and selflessness. Because of this, "retirement involvement" has its opposite, which we can call "retirement me-ism." Jim Conway frames "me-ism" in these sentiments:

> I've worked hard all my life. I obeyed my parents when I was a little kid. . . . I became respectable in the community . . . was a member of the PTA, the JayCees, and the local church board. . . . I've paid for braces, piano lessons, four different stages of bicycles. . . . I'm tired of doing all this. It's time that *I* get pleasure out of life. It's time for *me* to indulge *myself.* . . . *I'm* going to start using money for *my*

pleasure, *my* own leisure, to get *me* the kind of freedom
I want.[14]

Though we may not like to admit it, we can all identify with
those feelings. It's simple selfishness, and it can creep into our
thinking and flavor our attitudes without our even being aware
of it.

One of the effects of this kind of thinking is described by
Abraham Heschel in his book *The Insecurity of Freedom:*

> The pre-occupation with games and hobbies, the over-
> emphasis upon recreation, while certainly conducive to
> eliminating boredom temporarily, hardly contribute to in-
> ner-strength. The effect is rather a pickled existence pre-
> served in brine and spices.[15]

Though "retirement me-ism" can at times look very appetiz-
ing, we need to see it for what it is—a "pickled existence." It
has no life; therefore, it can bring forth no life.

Risk Something!

The other important ingredient in retiring *to* something is
the element of risk—risk that forces you to grow!

In an earlier chapter, I mentioned Stan Jameson, who
retired from his accounting business in Canada. His desire was
to combine his years of experience in accounting and business
management with an active role in Christian ministry. Stan
put it this way: "To me the big question was how could I fill
my life with something more than busyness?" For Stan, traveling or sports activities—even volunteer work—were not
enough. "The element that was missing in all these activities
was risk. To have a challenging, fulfilling life one needs to risk
something. Stan needed to commit himself to growth and with
it the tension between success and failure. "I decided to equip
myself for a specific task and learn something in addition to my
trade. The volunteer can have his little toe in a task without
too much commitment. I needed something that involved a
declaration of my ability to perform."

That commitment took Stan to theological seminary (*after*
retirement), and he hopes soon to be on the staff of a church

or other Christian organization, combining his skills in business
with his theological training.

When we commit ourselves to learning, growing, and productivity, of course, we also accept the possibility of missing
the mark. We risk failure. Yet it is this very element of risk that
brings a measure of meaning to life. Very little of worth is
accomplished in life without setting a goal, making a commitment, and "going for all the marbles."

You might say, "Well, I've never been that kind of a person."
But if you're holding a job and earning a living, you're involved
in risk every day! You place your training and ability on the
line every time you go to work. There's always the possibility
of failure, right? But you believe in your abilities. You *want* to
contribute to the success of your company. You believe you're
worth your keep, so every day you risk showing up and facing
the day's challenges.

The whole enterprise of raising children means involvement
in considerable risk. Decisions must constantly be made—
many times in the face of uncertainty and fear. The stakes are
high. Yet it is this very factor that forces us to search ourselves,
to reach out to others, to reach out to God for help and
strength. We are forced to learn and grow. And through it all,
we see our lives making a difference, at work, at home—and
it's well worth the risk. Life has meaning.

> What is risk? I risk when I live on the edge of my personal
> and social frontiers. And risking means expanding and ex-
> tending those frontiers so that we and the world we live
> in become larger and more interesting. The meaning of
> life becomes more exciting and worth exploring. Persons
> were created to grow; a non-growing person is a contra-
> diction.[16]

Cardinal Newman said: "We are so constituted that if we
insist upon being as sure as is conceivable, in every step of our
course, we must be content to creep along the ground, and can
never soar."[17] And in *The Will to Believe,* William James said:
"It is only by risking our persons from one hour to another that
we live at all."[18]

Indeed, the sad epitaph of too many retired people is that
they equate retirement with retreat. Instead of retiring to the

involvement, risk, and growth of *something*, they retire to the isolation, safety, and decay of *nothing*.

Today Is a Good Day to Begin

Begin your planning now to retire *to* something. In fact, it really should be to *many* things—a good mix of recreational hobbies, work, and ministry involvement. Plan for it just as you would plan for entering a new business—for, in one sense, that's precisely what you're doing.

If you're interested in a "second career," perhaps you should gain your organization's permission (if needed) to start experimenting with that career or business now. Most businesses, crafts, and hobbies have their own newsletters and journals. Go to the local library and find out what they are, and start subscribing to them.

Sit down with your wife or husband (or a close friend), and dream a little. What do you enjoy doing? What have you often dreamed about, but never dared to pray about—or plan for?

John F. Kennedy said, "There are risks and costs to a program of action. But they are far less than the long-range risks and costs of comfortable inaction."[19]

Right now, risk dreaming—risk believing—risk praying—risk planning.

You can't lose!

Source Notes

1. Quoted in Jerome Ellison, *Life's Second Half* (Old Greenwich, Conn., The Devin-Adair Co., Inc., 1978), p. 23.
2. Quoted in Edmund LeBreton, *Plan Your Retirement Now So You Won't Be Sorry Later* (Washington, D.C.: U. S. News & World Report Publishers, 1974), p. 47.
3. Robert C. Benedict, "Preparing for Retirement: Crisis or Challenge?" Hearing Before the Sub-committee on Retirement Income and Employment of the Select Committee on Aging, House of Representatives, Ninety-fifth Congress, Second Session (Washington, D.C.: U. S. Government Printing Office, 1978), p. 50.

4. Ted W. Engstrom and David J. Juroe, *The Work Trap* (Old Tappan, N.J.: Fleming H. Revell Company, 1979), p. 34.
5. Smiley Blanton, *Now or Never* (Englewood Cliffs, N.J.: Prentice-Hall, Inc. 1959), p. 85.
6. "Retirees' Advice: Stay Out of the Easy Chair," *U. S. News & World Report,* February 26, 1979, p. 62.
7. Louis Harris and Associates, Inc., *1979 Study of American Attitudes Toward Pension and Retirement* (New York: Johnson Higgins, 1979), p. ix.
8. Quoted in "Retirees' Advice: Stay Out of the Easy Chair," op. cit., p. 62.
9. Jeffrey Sonnenfeld, "Dealing With the Aging Work Force," *Harvard Business Review,* November-December 1978, p. 88.
10. Robert J. Ahrens, "Retirement, Work, and Lifelong Learning," Hearing Before the Special Committee on Aging, United States Senate, Ninety-fifth Congress, Second Session (Washington, D.C.: U. S. Government Printing Office, 1978), p. 229.
11. Reuel L. Howe, *How to Stay Younger While Growing Older* (Waco, Tex.: Word, Inc., 1974), p. 131–32.
12. "Creative Retirement," *The Royal Bank of Canada Monthly Newsletter,* September 1978.
13. Stan Vaughn, "These Bugs Have Him Fit to Be Tied," *The Napa* (Calif.) *Register,* February 23, 1980, p. 2A.
14. Jim Conway, *Men in Mid-Life Crisis* (Elgin, Ill.: David C. Cook Publishing Company, 1978), p. 130.
15. Quoted in Leland F. Cooley and Lee Morrison Cooley, *How to Avoid the Retirement Trap* (Los Angeles: Nash Publishing Corporation, 1972), p. 219.
16. Howe, op. cit., p. 29.
17. John Henry Cardinal Newman, in *The Crown Treasury of Relevant Quotations,* Edward F. Murphy, ed. (New York: Crown Publishers, Inc., 1978), p. 512.
18. William James, in *The Crown Treasury of Relevant Quotations,* p. 512.
19. John F. Kennedy, in *The Crown Treasury of Relevant Quotations,* p. 6.

9
The Health Factor

He who has health has hope; and he who has hope has everything.

ARAB PROVERB

The possibility of poor health is one of the greatest concerns people have relative to retirement: "Will I be strong enough, aware enough, and healthy enough to enjoy it?"

Certainly, there is nothing that could more quickly ruin the better half of your life than poor health and the attendant burdens of huge medical bills.

Fortunately, though, this gloomy picture is not the *complete* picture. For most of us, there are reasons to be optimistic. For example, the American Medical Association has stated that there are no diseases *of* the aged—simply diseases *among* the aged.[1] That would seem to say that aging and poor health should not be considered one and the same.

And again:

> The myth about aging and illness must be dispelled once and for all. Most diseases are not synonymous with getting older, although stress and sickness can accelerate an aging syndrome. Let's consider cerebral blood flow and oxygen consumption for instance. Tests have proven that there is no significant difference between normal, healthy twenty-one year old men and healthy men between ages sixty-five and ninety![2]

If You're Going to Use It, Maintain It!

But if this is true, why is poor health so common in advanced years? The overwhelming evidence seems to point to poor maintenance as the reason! Maintaining physical and mental health is evidently much like maintaining an automobile: abuse and neglect will subtract years from your life, just as they will from your car. Therefore, *illness is not so much the result of aging itself, as it is the result of accumulated years of poor maintenance:* poor diet, overeating, other bad habits, overweight, lack of exercise, and the lack of concern for proper rest and regular medical checkups. "Burning the candle at both ends" finally takes its toll.

There is close to universal agreement on the broad guidelines of this necessary maintenance. The three basic rules that doctors say should be followed are: eat properly, and in moderation; get enough exercise; have regular physical examinations. Preventive medicine is the best medicine.

The problem is that these directives are so familiar—for most of us, they go back at least to kindergarten—that we effectively put them aside once we become "adults." ("When I was a child I thought as a child.") All too often, it takes a major illness, such as a heart attack, to wake us up to the realization: "I guess my body *is* important, and I'd better take better care of it after all!"

I sincerely hope that you won't wait that long, but will take advantage of some of the suggestions in this chapter. For instance, consider the fact that 86 percent of all people 65 and over die of coronary artery disease (arteriosclerosis). Yet this is a disease most doctors believe can be controlled, at least to some degree, by proper diet and exercise begun in one's twenties.[3]

"But I'm not in my twenties," you say. All the more reason, then, to begin improving your health *now.* The secret of good health in retirement, all things being equal, is a matter of the right exercise and diet throughout your younger—and especially your middle—years.

There is perhaps no subject where the saying, "What you will be, you are now becoming," is as pertinent as with the subject of mental and physical health. Good health cannot be deferred, filed under Begin at Retirement. In too many cases, that will be too late. The "hows" of good health need to be put into action *now.*

Keep Your Mind Exercised and Fed

I've stated several times already that poor physical health can often be directly traced to poor mental health. George Bernard Shaw was quite correct when he said, "All sorts of bodily diseases are produced by half-used minds."[4]

Keeping your mind flexible and active is absolutely vital. If the mind is not used—"stretched"—it can grow slack and lethargic.

> This process is aided by the myth that the mental faculties of human beings start declining sharply after a certain age. In fact, one group of American psychologists has found that the mind does not achieve its fullest powers until the age of 60 and declines only very slowly thereafter.[5]

Of course, keeping the mind active is something that has to become a way of life—beginning now. We cannot turn on some magical switch at age 65, and reverse the poor thinking habits of a lifetime. This is where the area of enjoyable work, hobbies, reading, and involvement with others is invaluable. David Ray observes:

> Middle-agers are prone to suffer from what I call "mental-sclerosis"—a hardening of the intellectual, scholastic, learning arteries. Yet a closed mind is a contradiction. Very little goes in, but lots of things are forever coming out.[6]

This is really the cause of "senility." As we discussed in our chapter on aging, senility is not a "disease of the aged": it is the result of *mental retirement:*

> Manifestations of it can develop in men or women in the 40s when they become affluent enough to cease working and begin pampering themselves. They establish a self-centered routine—and coast.[7]

It is important, therefore, to keep our minds exercised and sensibly fed.

Bring Order to Your Life

There is another thing that can break down good mental health. That is the lack of an ordered life—the lack of goals, and a scale of priorities among those goals. As indicated earlier, goals—at any age in life—are highly motivational. Goal setting and goal achievement are most fulfilling and rewarding:

> As any doctor can attest, hospitals and medical waiting rooms are jammed with people whose physical ailments stem from division within themselves. Disorganization and lack of goals can produce psychosomatic illness—*stress diseases,* the experts call them—because when body, mind, and spirit fail to function in harmony, illness results.[8]

Setting up priorities for the activities and duties of life may sound extremely difficult. However, it often means nothing more than forcing yourself to simply sit down with a sheet of paper and make a list. (Somehow, those myriads of details spinning around in your head lose much of their power to confuse and frustrate when regarded in black and white.) The next step is to make some decisions about priority, based on the value you place on each item and the time you have to accomplish the various tasks.

Goals are always important. Ideally, they should include not only those things you feel you *should* accomplish, but things you simply enjoy doing. You should set some "rewards" out there for yourself—for tomorrow, for next week, next month, next year. There are some excellent books on goal setting, and on managing your time in such a way as to realize them.

No Matter *What* You Think, You *Are* What You Think

Finally, what you fill your mind with is a key to your mental health. No doubt about it, you are what you think. This has been rightly emphasized in the many "positive thinking" books published in the past few years. However, as is so often the case, the Bible said it first (and best): Philippians 4:4–8 (NAS) is unsurpassed when it comes to a true, scriptural prescription for "positive thinking":

Rejoice in the Lord always; again I will say, rejoice! Let your forbearing spirit be known to all men. The Lord is near. Be anxious for nothing, but in everything by prayer and supplication with thanksgiving let your requests be made known to God. And the peace of God, which surpasses all comprehension, shall guard your hearts and your minds in Christ Jesus. Finally, brethren, whatever is true, whatever is honorable, whatever is right, whatever is pure, whatever is lovely, whatever is of good repute, if there is any excellence and if anything worthy of praise, let your mind dwell on these things. . . . and the God of peace shall be with you.

The most important ingredient of good mental health—and one that must be developed now, not upon retirement—is having "the God of peace with you." And that comes as you commit yourself to a vital, moment-by-moment relationship with God. Time spent soaking in God's Word—time spent in worship of and a personal relationship with your Heavenly Father is the most valuable time you can spend. It is here that you will be able to get in touch with your true identity and your true purpose for being alive. It is here you will gain the confidence and spiritual resources it takes to bring fulfillment *to* life.

You Are What You Eat!

Probably nothing should be more obvious to us than the importance of diet in maintaining physical health. Yet much of the time we act as if we believe that eating and good health have little in common. Slowly, however, this situation seems to be changing: more and more Americans are realizing the vital importance of better nutritional eating habits.

Senator George McGovern has reported:

Cancer, stroke and heart disease—this Nation's major killers—are not the inevitable tolls of aging; . . . six of the ten leading causes of death are nutrition related, and . . . their debilitating impact is felt most directly among older Americans; . . . a better diet can improve one's health at any stage of the aging process.[9]

For Americans over 45, the leading causes of illness and death are heart disease, cancer, stroke, accidents and cirrhosis of the liver.[10] In addition to poor nutrition, there are other physical habits that contribute to these illnesses. For instance, your chances of heart disease; lung, mouth, and throat cancer; and emphysema are reduced considerably if you don't smoke. And many deaths directly or indirectly attributed to accidents, coronary problems, and "natural causes" are, in fact, caused by drinking.

Death from heart disease—to say nothing of the lowered resistance that opens the door to numerous infections—can be brought on by long years of eating the wrong foods, or eating the wrong combinations of foods, or the wrong quantities. Alcohol, nicotine, caffeine, sugar, saturated fats, the heavy cholesterol foods (eggs, chocolate, dairy foods), and heavily salted foods are items that should be kept to a minimum, if not dropped entirely from the diet. Fresh fruits and vegetables, whole grains, lean animal proteins (fish, fowl, meat), and dried nuts are among the most beneficial foods and may be eaten in generous quantities.

> Your body is constantly changing, trying to maintain, repair, and rebuild itself. Yet most people don't give it much help. By supplying the necessary reconstruction materials, you can help to perpetuate good health. . . .[11]

The American public is becoming increasingly aware of the fact that far too little actual food value is offered by the average American diet of highly processed foods. The real definition of "food" is not, after all, just that which fills the stomach, but that which is taken into the body for *nourishment.* We don't have to be "health nuts" to figure out that the irregular and rushed eating of "plastic" junk foods, soft drinks, and desserts doesn't do much to maintain the physical machine. The right combination of proteins, carbohydrates, and fats is necessary for the body to repair itself and produce the energy you need, and will continue to need in the years to come.

My purpose here is not so much to recommend a daily regimen as to alert you to the tremendous importance of your diet. I encourage you, therefore, to go to a health-food store and purchase a couple of good books on health and nutrition. Your small investment will be amply returned to you in the form of good health in your retirement years.

No one need remind you that keeping your weight in control is also important for good health. Arnold H. Glasgow reminds us that our body is the baggage we carry through life—the more excess baggage, the shorter the trip.[12] If you are considerably overweight, you run *two to three times* the risk of heart disease as a person of normal weight.

Also, because our bodies are temples of the Holy Spirit, created by God, there are some very real spiritual implications to our eating habits.

> Prayer before eating should be more than a ritual; it should be a statement of obedience to God that we will eat what He wants us to eat, and the amount that He tells us! Sensitivity to His leading in this important area will have the direct result of increased awareness and vitality.[13]

Just Joggin' Along

Bob Mockler says that "middle age is when you're not inclined to exercise anything but caution."[14] Yet it's pretty hard to drive through suburban America on the way to work these mornings without seeing one or two near mid-lifers in full sweatsuit jogging down the street. It is a positive and encouraging trend in our country. The usual reaction as we drive by in the car, however, is to say to ourselves: "I really ought to try that; it'd be good for me! Think I'll start tomorrow." But tomorrow always turns out to be a day "down the road."

The importance of physical activity—or the lack of it—and its connection with heart disease were given support by a classic study conducted among British postal workers. It was demonstrated that those doing desk jobs suffered a higher incidence *of*—and mortality *from*—heart attacks than did their more active colleagues employed in "strenuous" mail delivery![15]

Jerome Ellison says that most Americans are "overfed, under-oxygenated, and under-exercised."[16] Doctors agree, and say that exercising delays the deterioration of physical and mental abilities; makes the blood circulate faster; keeps the heart and lungs strong; improves the digestion; keeps the limbs active; reduces mental fatigue and tension; and even tends to increase self-confidence. Now, those are some pretty solid benefits—so why don't we do it?

Some of us don't begin regular physical activity or exercising because we feel it's too late. Sheldon MacDonald, who I mentioned in an earlier chapter, was challenged at age 48. Though Sheldon kept no regular program of physical exercise, he went hiking one weekend in the High Sierras with some Scouts, then followed this up with a spur-of-the-moment game of tennis. Two days later, when he went for his annual physical checkup and reported the mountain-climbing and tennis feats, his doctor said, "You're crazy!" Sheldon thought this meant the doctor had found something wrong with his heart. But the doctor said, "No, for a 48-year-old heart that isn't used to regular exercise, you're pretty normal. But with your impromptu games of tennis and the like—there *will* be a problem, unless you get in shape!"

Sheldon asked his doctor what he could do to *get* in shape, and the doctor told him to begin jogging barefoot in the house, from room to room, or even around the room, for 20 minutes a day. (Sheldon calls it "feeble jogging"!) Six months later, Sheldon went back to his doctor and went on the treadmill: that simple discipline had brought his heartbeat down to the high 50s. That was more than fifteen years ago, and in those fifteen years Sheldon has climbed most of the lower peaks in Southern California.

Though Sheldon's exercise program doesn't consist of running three miles a day, he is consistent in the program he has chosen—and that's very important. Incidentally, Sheldon likes this program because business trips never deter him from his exercising. "I wish I had a dollar for every Holiday Inn I've jogged in!" he says.

This example brings up an important point about beginning a physical exercise program. Too many people try to jump into a regimen that is so strenuous at the outset that it's given up after the third day. Or, they feel that in order to begin a program of regular exercise, they must learn some sport that they really don't enjoy.

Perhaps you enjoy running two or three miles—or more— every day. If so, more power to you! However, there are other ways to exercise, including some less strenuous. Here's a mix to consider: swimming, golf, bowling, tennis, calisthenics, handball, mountain climbing, boating, racquetball, and hiking. Even housework and gardening can be good physical exercise, and many doctors say that a good, brisk walk at a faster-than-normal pace is just about the best kind of exercise you can get.

Boston's Dr. Paul Dudley White, the acknowledged "dean of world cardiologists," said, "The kind of exercise is not very important except that it should suit the strength, aptitude, and liking of the particular person."[17]

Two final points are important in building good health: First, get enough rest. *You* know how much sleep you need, whether that be nine hours or four hours. Again, it is easy to take this point too lightly. Rather than following the rules for good health, it is somehow easier to drive ourselves—even in beneficial Christian service—without considering the damage we are doing to ourselves in the meantime. Saint Vincent de Paul said, "It is a trick of the devil, which he employs to deceive good souls, to incite them to do more than they are able, in order that they may no longer be able to do anything."[18]

Choose your priorities, and put your body up there high on the list. Without that, you *won't* be available for anything.

Finally, one of the best ways to avoid health problems is with regular medical checkups. Especially if you are over 40, be sure to make this an annual event!

Why Not Get Serious—Now!

Much of what I've said in this chapter has to do with coming to grips with the importance of the gift of life and health that God has given to you, and having the courage to make some decisions that will make a big difference in the years to come. I know these aren't easy decisions—especially when you're talking about lifelong habits of overeating and underexercising. "But you have to make it a *be* attitude. You have to *be*-gin, have to *be* up-and-going, have to *be* in control."[19]

It's quite humbling to realize that we can do precious little in this world—for God, for man, or for ourselves—without the proper functioning of this miraculous "building" in which God has placed each of us. As Henry Miller said: "Our own body possesses a wisdom which we who inhabit the body lack. We give it orders which make no sense."[20]

Take control of your body—now. Begin giving it the right "orders"—and the proper care. Begin to order your life and fill your thoughts with the stuff that will make you the person you want to be. Be a bit more of a "health nut"—for your own and your retirement's sake—and start a regular program of exercise.

What are the benefits?

Life . . . the feeling of good health . . . and the ability to enjoy your retirement years to the full!

That ought to be enough for starters!

I urge you therefore, brethren, by the mercies of God, to present your bodies a living and holy sacrifice, acceptable to God, which is your spiritual service of worship. And do not be conformed to this world, but be transformed by the renewing of your mind, that you may prove what the will of God is, that which is good and acceptable and perfect.

Romans 12:1, 2, ASV

Or do you not know that your body is a temple of the Holy Spirit who is in you, whom you have from God, and that you are not your own? For you have been bought with a price. Therefore glorify God in your body.

1 Corinthians 6:19, 20 NAS

Source Notes

1. David Ray, *The Forty Plus Handbook* (Waco, Tex.: Word, Inc., 1979), p. 47.
2. M. Shrout, M. Burnett, and M. Gifford, *Senior Adult Leadership Handbook* (Jenkintown, Pa.: Louis Neibauer Co., Inc., 1976), p. 43.
3. Lee Butcher, *Retirement Without Fear* (Princeton, N. J.: Dow Jones Books, 1978), p. 101.
4. George Bernard Shaw, in *The Crown Treasury of Relevant Quotations,* Edward F. Murphy, ed. (New York: Crown Publishers, Inc., 1978), p. 347.
5. "Creative Retirement," *The Royal Bank of Canada Monthly Newsletter,* September 1978, p. 3.
6. Ray, op. cit., pp. 29, 30.

7. Oren Arnold, *The Second Half of Life* (Irvine, Calif.: Harvest House Publishers, 1979), p. 66.

8. Charlotte Hale Allen, *Full-Time Living* (Old Tappan, N.J.: Fleming H. Revell Company, 1978), p. 86.

9. George McGovern, "Diet Related to Killer Diseases, VII," Hearing Before the Select Committee on Nutrition and Human Needs of the United States Senate, Ninety-fifth Congress, First Session (Washington, D.C.: U. S. Government Printing Office, 1979), p. 1.

10. Tony Lamb and Dave Duffy, *The Retirement Threat* (Los Angeles: J. P. Tarcher, Inc., 1977), p. 95.

11. Linda Clark, *Secrets of Health and Beauty* (New York: Pyramid Books, 1970), p. 16.

12. Quoted in *Reader's Digest*, October 1976, p. 486.

13. Raymond and Anne Ortlund, *The Best Half of Life* (Glendale, Calif.: Regal Books, 1976), p. 46.

14. Ibid.

15. Alexander Leaf, "Everyday Is a Gift When You're Over 100," *National Geographic*, January 1974, p. 110.

16. Jerome Ellison, *Life's Second Half* (Old Greenwich, Conn., The Devin-Adair Co., Inc., 1978), p. 108.

17. Quoted in Leland F. Cooley and Lee Morrison Cooley, *How to Avoid the Retirement Trap* (Los Angeles: Nash Publishing Corporation, 1972), p. 209.

18. Saint Vincent de Paul, in *The Crown Treasury of Relevant Quotations*, p. 346.

19. Arnold, op. cit., p. 100.

20. Henry Miller, in *The Crown Treasury of Relevant Quotations*, p. 97.

10

Investing in Relationships

Do not protect yourself by a fence, but rather by your friends.

CZECH PROVERB

There is no way to measure the value of friendship. Have you ever stopped to consider how many friends you have? Do you have the important knack of cultivating friendships? Or do you stand apart, knowing many people casually, but never taking the time to build those deeper relationships that could reap rich rewards in your retirement years?

Saint Alfred of Rievaulx said that "No medicine is more valuable, none more efficacious, none better suited to the cure of all our temporal ills than a friend, to whom we may turn for consultation in time of trouble, and with whom we may share our happiness in time of joy."[1]

If you are prepared, your retirement years can provide a tremendous opportunity to enjoy the dividends of long friendships. For one thing, close friends will be even more appreciated during those years: God has ordained that, as the years pass, we become more capable of seeing the value of relationships that have been seasoned with time.

Horace Walpole wrote: "Old friends are the great blessing of one's later years—half a word conveys one's meaning. They have memory of the same events and have the same mode of thinking . . . ."[2]

Do you have a friend—or, better, friends—like that?

Invest in Friends Now—You'll Need Them Later

Besides *enjoying* such friendships, it is important to realize that during your retirement years you'll almost certainly *need* them. UCLA psychiatrist Roger Gould sees hunger for personal relationships a prime factor of aging:

Imbued with the idea that adults once adult, are never supposed to change, people tend to be badly shaken at finding themselves different from what they were a decade or two earlier. Trouble arises when they try to deny these changes instead of accepting, comprehending, and learning from them. The best way to learn, of course, is through creative interchange with intelligent peers undergoing similar changes and coping with them.[3]

There can be little meaning in life without relationships with others. First, of course, our relationships with God our Creator; then, with significant others. In *Prime Time,* Herb Barks says:

Our search for meaning begins with *choices.* We must decide what will be our source of meaning. We must decide where we are going to look for meaning. We must set a priority on the person-to-person times in our lives.[4]

In relating work and relationships to meaning, Barks goes on to say:

What I suggest is that you not worry about where you are in the company, that you put aside your need to achieve and find meaning. Instead, look to the Lord and the people that stand in the shadows of your life, and see if perhaps there you might find what you search for day after day.[5]

So friendships are not only a great source of fulfillment in retirement, but they are also sorely needed. And, of course, it goes without saying that if a treasury of meaningful friendships are to be yours to enjoy during retirement, they must be "in process" now—because friendships take time to cultivate and bring to maturity.

What's a Friend?

But what do we really mean when we talk about "having friends"? Let's take a look at that question.

We all realize that there are different kinds of friendships—some very casual, others quite intimate. In his book, *Communications: Key to Marriage,* Christian psychologist H. Norman Wright talks about five levels of interpersonal communications.[6] Understanding these levels can help to evaluate the quality of our friendships. Wright begins with the fifth level which he calls "cliché conversation"—the everyday social conversation with those we meet casually, on the street or at the supermarket. The "How are you?", "How's the family?", "How's the job?" sort of thing—"safe" conversation, in which there is virtually no personal sharing.

Level four is "reporting the facts about others." This involves talking about what others have said, but without any personal commentary. Every such conversation consists, essentially, of a "Five O'clock News" report of what happened today and what So-and-so said.

Level three includes "our personal ideas and judgment." Here is where some meaningful communication begins. At this level, we are willing to step out of our solitary confinement and risk revealing some of our inner ideas and concerns.

Level two is "our feelings or emotions." This is when we express how we feel about those facts, ideas, and judgments. Again, we are revealing even more about who we are and what we believe.

Level one is "complete emotional and personal truthful communication." All deep relationships—and especially marriage—must be built on this kind of absolute openness and honesty.

> This may be difficult to achieve because it involves a risk—
> the risk of being rejected because of our honesty. . . . There
> will be times when this type of communication is achieved
> and other times when the communication is not as com-
> plete as it could be.[7]

Our goal should be to cultivate a variety of friends with whom we communicate at different levels of openness and intimacy. It is normal to have a greater number of friends with whom we communicate at levels five and four, rather than at the very personal and open level one. (Most relationships begin at level five and four before it is possible to move deeper.)

Our real problem, however, is that in our very mobile and impersonal society, it is easy to know large numbers of people, with whom we never move beyond a "How's the work, the wife, the kids?" level of communication (levels five and four). In fact, we can know people for years—at work, at church— and never get beyond this level. Such cliché conversations cannot be considered the stuff out of which lasting friendships are made. If most of your friendships are at this level, you will find yourself entering retirement destitute of the kind of sustaining, enriching relationships that you will need—and that you could be enjoying now.

The Foundation for Friendship

There is no context that lends itself more readily to the cultivation of deep friendships than the church. True friendship is based, after all, on love for one another. Jesus said, "This is My commandment, that you love one another, just as I have loved you" (John 15:12 NAS).

Wonderfully, God has given us the resources with which to fulfill that commandment, a commandment given for our benefit and fulfillment.

Listen, too, to the Apostle Peter:

> For as you know him better, he will give you, through his great power, everything you need for living a truly good life. . . . Learn to put aside your own desires so that you will become patient and godly, gladly letting God have his way with you. This will make possible the next step which is for you to enjoy other people and to like them, and finally you will grow to love them deeply.
>
> 2 Peter 1:3, 6, 7 LB

The love of God has been sown within our hearts, providing God's great resource for building lasting, fulfilling relationships. So we of all people, as Christians, have the resources for lasting friendship.

Of course, God's love in our hearts should also move us out beyond the church walls. Friends outside our immediate racial, religious, economic, and social settings can help keep us "on the grow." Not only can we as Christians be "salt" in these relationships, but these friends can broaden and stimulate our thinking, open our eyes to the needs of others, and add new dimensions of interest and zest to our lives.

In short, a variety of friends, whom we appreciate and admire for a variety of reasons, is a good and healthy thing!

Three Hindrances to Gaining Friends

There are three things that can hinder our developing the friendships we desire. One is letting our Christian faith become more dogma or cold creed than the loving, vital relationship with Jesus Christ it ought to be. The life of Jesus, which manifests itself in love, is brought about by an openness, a yieldedness, an availability to His life (His Spirit) within us. If, through disobedience, neglect, or unbelief, that openness—and thus, that "life"—is quenched, love will be quenched. We will tend to *withdraw into ourselves.*

The second thing that can hinder our developing friendships is the fear that we won't be accepted. This fear can be imbedded deep within our personality—perhaps rooted in actual experiences in the past. If serious enough, personal counsel is needed to free a person from the grip of this fear. However, millions of Christian believers down through the centuries have given testimony to the fact that growing in an understanding of God's love for us—and an openness to His life in us—can conquer even the deepest fears. "Beloved, if God so loved us, we also ought to love one another. . . . *There is no fear in love; but perfect love casts out fear.* . . . We love, because He first loved us" (1 John 4:11, 18, 19 NAS, italics added).

One of the most consistent traits of people who have newly become Christians, and thus have a uniquely fresh sense of God's forgiveness, is an overwhelming love for others. The great message of Christianity down through the ages has been that because God loves us we can love ourselves—and thus love others. God's love frees us from fear!

The Gaithers' song says it so well:

> I am loved, I am loved,
> I can risk loving you,
> For the One who knows me best,
> Loves me most.[8]

The third hindrance in developing friendships is that we are not willing to take the first step ourselves—sometimes for the two reasons given above. The biblical principle is true: if we want friends, we must show ourselves friendly. We need to believe that God has *given* us His love as the ultimate resource for friendship, and that because of this, deep friendships can be ours. Then we need to risk possessing that which He has given.

Husband and Wife—Best Friends?

It might seem strange that I didn't begin this chapter on friendship by considering the marriage relationship. Certainly, if we are married, that is the relationship closest to our heart, and the most crucial during our retirement years.

However, I wanted you to look at the husband/wife relationship in the light of the importance and meaning of friendship —simply because friendship is one of the most important ingredients in marriage, particularly during retirement years.

It is surprising how many older marriages are in trouble. We used to feel that if a marriage had survived 20 or 30 years, there was proven stability. Not so any more. Many of these long-term marriages fall apart because the couple has little in common. They had children too early, before they really had the opportunity to become friends, only lovers. After the passion of love subsided, they looked for substitutes, perhaps in a job or other people. Now when they are older, they try too hard to have some kind of relationship. In my opinion, the basis for that relationship needs to be friendship.

Families today have fewer children, and it is not uncommon for children to be "out of the nest" while Mom and Dad are still in their 40s. Many a husband and wife have found themselves at this point in life, with tremendous expectations of what life will now be like, only to find that they don't have much of a marriage, because they have done very little during the past 20 years or so to improve the *quality* of their marriage.

What Really Happens?

Jim Conway points out four major problems that contribute to the breakdown of the marriage relationship in mid-life.[9] These can be considered clear warnings and positive points for improvement to any couple who wants to prepare now for fulfilling relationships during the retirement years.

The first is *preoccupation with the process of living*—giving priority to work, raising the kids, paying the mortgage, accumulating *things*, at the expense of getting to know one another better.

In this connection, I should add that, in this process of living, time is not always on our side. It is not necessarily a happy thought, but we should face the fact that, in and of itself, time can be a corrosive influence in a marriage. My dear friends Ray and Anne Ortlund remind us:

> We don't naturally drift closer together; we drift further apart. We have to fight our way back to each other, day after day, year after year, as long as we live.[10]

The second major problem area is *lack of communication and intimacy*. This means trying to carry on a marriage relationship while communicating no deeper than levels five and four (cliché conversation; reporting the facts about others). Many a husband and wife, though married 20 or 30 years, seldom if ever share their real feelings and emotions, and rarely talk to each other about how they *feel* toward each other, or about their goals and aspirations.

The third major threat to the mid-life marriage relationship is *unmet personal needs*. Many husbands and wives have vocational, social, intellectual, and/or emotional needs that they have never revealed to another person—or not until the problems in the relationship are so serious that a marriage counselor finally ferrets them out (sometimes in time to save the marriage).

The fourth problem area is *lack of personal growth*. As we have mentioned earlier, to keep life interesting and alive we need to keep growing. The same goes for the marriage relationship. We need to keep learning, and growing, not only together but as individuals:

> God has designed the human personality with a great potential for growth. If both people in the marriage are growing, there should never come a time when they know all there is to know about each other. Their relationship will remain fresh, and there won't be the likelihood of boredom.[11]

Turn Your Marriage Around

If you see any of the problems above making inroads into your marriage relationship, don't wait for it to improve—automatically—"with time." On the contrary, it will get worse, unless you take the steps now to turn things around. And you can!

You can make sure, for example, that you schedule times, preferably once a week, when you can talk intimately about things other than the day-to-day process of living. You need to share each other as persons—exchanging your real feelings about yourself, your dreams, your hopes, your concerns.

To do this, you might first have to do something you've never done before. Much conflict in marriage is caused by one party not being willing to admit his weaknesses, and his very real need of the other. This is especially true of the male of the species. It is one thing to be young and in love, and to tell your wife-to-be: "Darling, I need you." It is quite another to be 10 or 20 or 30 years into marriage, and—after years of trying to be the super-capable, super-"together" husband—finally remove the mask and admit that you desperately need your wife.

Robert Lee and Marjorie Casebier remind us:

> Security, and comfort of being stark-naked to at least one person in life before whom we can take off our masks, shed our psychological figleaf, and not have to pretend anymore. Such a relationship with a marriage partner can enable me to move more easily with others because someone knows my faults and still accepts me and cares for me, as well as frees me to realize my greater potential because I am not hung up on feeling guilty or stupid.[12]

In today's "macho" society, such an admission might be seen as a weakening of the husband's masculinity. In God's eyes, however, an honest, open, truthful admission of need reveals true strength of character. Blended with a willingness to forgive and accept and support, it is the stuff on which you can build an intimate, "level-one" husband-and-wife relationship.

Then Start Being Friends

Building on this foundation, I recommend that you and your spouse begin to do some of the kinds of things friends do. Begin to learn some activities and hobbies *together.* Tackle some home projects, or perhaps a church project, *together.* Then, plan regular times when the two of you just "kick around"— for example, a weekend away at a resort, or at least a night out to dinner (for sure, twice a month). Or take a drive, or regular walks, together. All of these things, done consistently during the mid-life years, are prime investments that will bring sizable dividends during your retirement.

One more thought:

> It's always worth remembering that the sexual joy of any couple can rarely transcend the general level of satisfaction that a husband and wife have with each other.[13]

Our Children—Are We Friends?

There has been much discussion of late about parents going overboard on being "friends"—rather than "just parents"—in relationship to their young children. Our focus here, however, is on the children of us middle-agers—the children who are just about ready to leave the nest (or have already flown). What about our relationship with *them* in the years to come?

Having a healthy, happy, continuing relationship will be important. But that, too, needs to be nurtured *now.* As parents of older children, one of the toughest hurdles for some of us is understanding that our "parenting" days are over.

> Children are not playthings, like sports cars, tennis rackets, or sailboats; they are persons. They are not our possessions. It is a man's responsibility from the moment of birth to move his children toward maturity and independence, to enable them to function at every age in life with confidence and effectiveness.[14]

It's not that in later life we aren't needed by our children; it's just that the ground rules are different. Our role now is to be supportive, while at the same time letting them lead their own lives. As difficult as that may be at times, you and they will be much happier if you do not impose your values or advice upon them, but rather wait to be asked. Not only will *you* be happier, but you will be closer to them, and better able to give counsel or help when they need it.

How then *should* we act—what *should* we do? (After all, they're still our children, even if they have children of their own.)

I would like to suggest that you be their friend. As much as possible, employ some of the same principles we talked about earlier in this chapter. Let them see you as a person, in addition to seeing you as a parent. This might involve some communication on levels three, two, and one. It might also involve taking some risks in revealing your needs and hopes and desires and—yes—your weaknesses. At the same time, let them know that you are always available to listen to, to talk with, to pray with them.

Another suggestion might be to get together in some activities and discussions other than family-related ones. (Here is where keeping your mind alive and growing will be important.) Being able to intelligently discuss current events; knowing something about your son-in-law's career; or "being up on" the latest best-seller can mean enjoyable hours spent with your children. Do all you can so that, in addition to being your children, they are your friends. Let me add, finally, drawing on my personal experience, what a sheer delight and joy such friendship is!

As You Would Have Men Do Unto You, Do Unto Them

A word should be said at this time about how we should treat our parents, who are perhaps in the closing years of life. Our attitude toward our parents should be based upon Exodus 20: 12: "Honor your father and mother, that you may have a long, good life in the land the Lord your God will give you" (LB). Elsewhere, Scripture exhorts us to heed a father's instruction, and not to forsake our mother's training (Proverbs 1:8; 4:1; 6:20).

Most of us would expend every effort to see that our parents are provided for during their twilight years. However, an often neglected step in truly "honoring" our parents is something very obvious and practical—simply, "keeping in touch":

> Nothing deadens Dad's and Mom's spirits quicker than careless children who don't communicate or try to understand and help with problems. . . . Begin making friends with your parents or aging relatives. Notice the startling difference in their dispositions in a short time. In fact, the extra bonus may just well be an improvement in their physical well-being, because a merry heart acts like medicine to the entire body.[15]

It is a fact that those who have remained close with their parents, allowing them to become friends and companions, are much more capable of coping with old age themselves. And because they have tried to understand and cultivate a close relationship with Mom and Dad, they are being obedient to the instructions of Exodus 20:12. It works!

Life's Meaning Is Not Found in Doing, But Rather in Relating

That's where it's at. Perhaps it is because God created *people* as His highest endeavor. He came to earth as a person. He came to relate to us, and to reveal to us the very nature of God, who is love.

His very coming, together with the reason for His dying and His living *now,* proves that people—others—are important. Vitally important. God came to earth to show us what love was all about, and to show us how to love one another.

> My loving may be rejected or betrayed. I can be hurt and disappointed by the response, but nothing and no one can take away from me the increase I experience because I love. Therefore, when I love, I am investing in the future of my becoming . . . .[16]

Begin investing in your future now, by getting to know other people . . . even your wife and children!

It's called relating. It's called friendship. It's called *abundant living* during your retirement years!

A true friend is always loyal, and a brother is born to help in time of need.

Proverbs 17:17 LB

Never abandon a friend—either yours or your father's. Then you won't need to go to a distant relative for help in your time of need.

Proverbs 27:10 LB

I have called you friends . . . .

John 15:15 NEB

Source Notes

1. Saint Alfred of Rievaulx, in *The Crown Treasury of Relevant Quotations,* Edward F. Murphy, ed. (New York: Crown Publishers, Inc., 1978), p. 305.
2. Horace Walpole, in *The Crown Treasury of Relevant Quotations,* p. 307.
3. Quoted in Jerome Ellison, *Life's Second Half* (Old Greenwich, Conn.: The Devin-Adair Co., Inc., 1978), p. 36.
4. Herb Barks, *Prime Time—Moving into Middle Age with Style* (Nashville, Tenn.: Thomas Nelson, Inc., 1978), p. 65.
5. Ibid.
6. H. Norman Wright, *Communication: Key to Marriage* (Glendale, Calif.: Regal Books, 1974), p. 68.
7. Ibid.
8. William J. and Gloria Gaither, "I Am Loved," Gaither Music Publishers, 1978.
9. Jim Conway, *Men in Mid-Life Crisis* (Elgin, Ill.: David C. Cook Publishing Company, 1978), p. 186.
10. Raymond and Anne Ortlund, *The Best Half of Life* (Glendale, Calif.: Regal Books, 1976), p. 97.
11. Conway, op. cit., p. 189.
12. Robert Lee and Marjorie Casebier, *The Spouse Gap* (Nashville, Tenn.: Abingdon Press, 1971), p. 64.
13. Ortlund, op. cit., p. 94.
14. Conway, op. cit., p. 250.
15. Peter Mustric, *The Joy of Growing Older* (Wheaton, Ill.: Tyndale House Publishers, 1979), p. 10.
16. Reuel L. Howe, *How to Stay Younger While Growing Older* (Waco, Tex.: Word, Inc., 1974), p. 47.

11
Future Trap

The present moment is significant not as the bridge between past and future, but by reason of its contents, which can fill our emptiness and become ours, if we are capable of receiving them.

DAG HAMMARSKJOLD

Thus far, we've considered some of the philosophical and practical aspects of planning for a fulfilling future. We've talked about the exciting opportunities presented by the retirement years. And we've discussed the potential pitfalls of heedlessly pointing our "ship of life" toward old age, setting our instruments on "automatic pilot," and hoping—without any preparation—to wake up one morning enjoying the security and fulfillment of "retirement harbor."

To help avoid the tragedy of such a course, we've outlined some specific moorings to help you navigate the stormy waters of mid-life crisis, aging, and death. Realizing, at the same time, that concepts are useless unless translated into action, we've discussed in practical terms just how to prepare for your retirement years in the areas of money, work, relationships, and health.

The emphasis has been upon the absolute necessity of planning now—not only to be a good steward of the years God has given you, but also to make sure your retirement years are the best years of your life.

In his book *How to Stay Younger While Growing Older*, Reuel L. Howe writes:

> Our insurance against tomorrow is what we do today. Your today may be a day in your thirty-fifth year; mine may be in my sixty-eighth—it matters not. . . . The kind of older person we become will be influenced by the way we live today.[1]

When N. W. Freeman, board chairman of Tenneco Inc., talks about the plans for his company he says, "We're positioned for the future."[2] The question we should each be asking ourselves is, "Am *I* positioned for the future?"

> God expects His people to think future—to be "positioned for the future." That's why He spoke to Joshua and said, "You are growing old . . . and there are still many nations to be conquered."[3]

God knew there were things to be accomplished in the future, and that Joshua needed to be aware of them and planning now.

Why the importance of "thinking and planning for the future"? Because of our human tendency either to live as though the future will never arrive (sometimes stemming from a fear of the future), or, through ignorance, to "back into" the future, without benefit of planning. Either approach robs us of enjoying all that God has provided for the second half of life.

The Hidden Future Trap

However, there exists still another kind of future trap, one that, ironically, lies hidden in the very thing we are advocating —that being, of course, preparedness for the future. For just as there is grave risk in not planning for the future, there is also danger in using the future as an excuse for not fully enjoying the present.

Unfortunately, human nature always seems to tend toward extremes. We seem always to be pulled toward one side of the pendulum, rather than taking the more difficult (if sometimes monotonous) course of keeping relatively steady and balanced at the center.

Those persons who constantly dream about the ideal life they will have "when they retire," or "when their ship comes in," or "when things get better," are deluding themselves. If there is any lasting truth that you receive through this book, I hope it is that *you cannot separate the future and the present.* We cannot live entirely in the present without destroying the future, nor entirely in the future without destroying the present.

In the final analysis, then, the goal can't be "getting a handle on the future," because the future cannot be an end in itself.

Balancing the Future With the Present

One thing that will help us achieve a balance between living in the present and looking ahead to the future is to see life as the continuity that it is.

> There is a certain continuity to your entire life—a continuity which moves with you from one stage of life into the next.[4]

But there's more to experiencing this continuity than just making wise decisions that will affect the future. What about the ability to actually enjoy the present? Without this capacity, our plans for the future are vain; we simply will not be able to enjoy it when it comes, but will always be hoping for tomorrow.

"Tomorrow, Tomorrow"

You remember when we were discussing the "sting of death," we said that the "sting" was fear: fear of death, fear of a future ending. We saw that this exhibits itself in our culture's herd-like mentality, that sees so many of us rushing about, trying to gain and have and experience it all before the "ruler of all"—Death—delivers the final blow. Success must be gained quickly, material goods must be acquired and accumulated *now,* "while they can still be enjoyed," because "the clock is ticking," and golden opportunities are slipping away. So, we should "get it while we can."

Though we Christians, possessing eternal life, should have a different outlook, we, too, can be seduced by this kind of "fear mentality." Such fear often expresses itself in an intense preoccupation with planning, earning, investing for the future. And it can be so subtly consuming that we soon find ourselves incapable of really enjoying the present. Our lives become wrapped up in tomorrow, while the present moment—the very essence of living, of life—is never captured.

The writer Anaïs Nin provides a very telling description of our generation in this regard:

> People do not live in the present always, at one with it.
> They live at all kinds of and manners of distance from it, as

difficult to measure as the course of the planets. Fears and traumas make their journeys slanted, peripheral, uneven and evasive.[5]

This can be all too true of both men and women of middle age. Jim Conway aptly describes the predicament of the former:

He is often so preoccupied with his past failures and future fears that he is unable to enjoy the now. Even though he feels an urgency to make something happen before it is too late, he fails to enjoy life as it comes. He doesn't enjoy his wife and family, his work, God, or nature and creation.[6]

Plan for the Future—but Live in the Present

How about you? In the midst of sincere concerns about the future of your family, work, finances, ministry, are you able to enjoy the moment—the here and now of life?

How about the little things (which can be so very big and meaningful)? How about the simple, everyday activities of life: going to work on a spring morning, sharing lunch and good conversation with friends, coming home to your family, even such a "trivial" action as opening the day's mail. Do you savor the joy of these simple events in your life?

How about the love you receive from your wife, children, and friends, and the joy of giving love back to them? Is that something that makes life worthwhile *now,* or are you too busy —perhaps worrying about the future—even to realize that the present with its many current joys is yours . . . *now!*

And, too, what about those little moments *within* the events and activities of living? How long has it been since you stopped on your way out to pick up the morning paper, paused and enjoyed the early morning freshness—and the wondrous fact that you are a part of it! How long has it been since you've enjoyed the beauty of a flower—or a moment of relaxation with a cup of coffee? Without, I hope, sounding like a television commercial, let me ask you if you've ever thought of enjoying the moment itself, as a part of life . . . *now?*

There are so many moments and experiences throughout an "average" day, moments to be savored just because they exist (and not because of the part they play in the great plans you have for the future).

> It is the privilege of living to be aware of a curtain's fold or the intonation of a human's voice. To be acutely, agonizingly conscious of the moment that is always present and always passing.[7]

Listen to André Gide:

> In order to be utterly happy the only thing necessary is to refrain from comparing this moment with other moments of the past—which I often did not fully enjoy because I was comparing them with other moments of the future.[8]

Ask yourself these questions. Do you find yourself living for the next moment, hour, week or year? Are you living for the time when, finally, you get "that raise," or "that house," or "that perfect job," or become "that better Christian," or "retire"?

Friend, if this is your pattern of thought and living, you're being dreadfully deceived! You are blindly entering the worst kind of "future trap." *It is only to the degree that you are able to enjoy the present moments of life that you will be able to enjoy your future.* The future does not contain within itself any miraculous elixir that will enable you to enjoy it. Enjoyment is an art that has to be learned in the present.

". . . But It's Tough to Live in the Present!"

It's very easy to fantasize about the future; it's sometimes very difficult to *live* in the present. Though our present may contain pleasure, laughter, contentment, we have to admit that, at times, it seems to contain much more frustration, conflict, pain, and just plain "tough sledding." So we're understandably tempted to turn our thoughts and efforts toward the future—when "it will all be different."

Somehow, though, we must reach peace in the present if we are to live in balance with the future, without having to use it as a "crutch."

We know that we cannot manipulate the events of our lives

so that everything always "comes up roses." We've all tried it, but it just doesn't work. No, we must go deeper: we must discover something that gives our present experiences— whether they be good or bad—meaning and significance.

And that something exists—but not in a pat formula or plan. It begins with, and is cultivated by, a vital relationship with a certain person—the creator of the universe, Jesus Christ.

We Christians often shortchange ourselves when it comes to appropriating all the resources that our Lord offers. We need to remind ourselves every day that we have Someone abiding within us who wants to be the comforting "constant" in our lives—if we will but rest in Him. You see, we have a Lord who is not limited by past, present, or future. He is the ". . . Alpha and Omega, the beginning and the end" (Revelation 21:6 NAS). He not only walks in our present experiences, but has already trod our future—retirement years and all. He is the "canopy" of life. He provides the continuity for life. He is the "Eternal Spirit" (Hebrews 9:14). And, best of all, He's ours!

It is because of this fact that He can provide meaning to our present moments. Even those difficult moments—the ones that contain far many more questions than answers.

To God Your Present Is As Important As Your Future

Jesus talked much about the future in His ministry. He talked about future events on earth, about eternal life, and even about the wisdom of planning for the future (Luke 14:28). However, He spent most of His days ministering to the urgent *present* needs of the men and women who sought out His teaching and His healing. And it's the same today: today, He is interested in meeting your present needs—because today is where your life is happening.

With God, the process of living is very important. That's because within the seemingly disconnected events of our lives, within those things that make us want to "escape" to the future, there is something else at work. Jim Conway points out:

> [In mid-life] the man believes the end product is the most important thing; the method of getting there is relatively unimportant. However, God seems to believe the process of moving through life is as important as the end result. So

Jesus encouraged us to trust our day by day affairs to God.
. . . That means God doesn't avoid pain to accomplish your
goal. He uses all of life, including pain, to help us develop
our character.[9]

*God is interested in developing you as a person—and He
uses present experience to do it.* He wants to build your character and mold you into His image. Sure, He has tremendous
plans for your future: in fact, you're going to live with Him in
perfection for all eternity! But it's His plan that that perfecting
should begin within the boundaries of time—in the present.
With Him—as it should be with us—there is a continuity between the present and the future. God brings meaning to the
seemingly unrelated events of our present lives!

Live in the Present and Enjoy It,
While Planning for the Future

If this God of unsurpassing love and faithfulness lives in our
hearts; if we know, further, that He can use every circum-
stance of life to build our character and make our life more
abundant; and if we also know, finally, that there is both a
present and an eternal purpose to our lives, then we can well
afford to be at peace and to begin enjoying life—*now!*

We, the forgiven—the redeemed-back-to-God—should be
the first to be savoring the experiences, the relationships, the
beauty God gives us in our present moments. So enjoy each
moment God gives you, for itself alone—*not* for what it might
bring you in the future. Then, express yourself in thankfulness
—to others, and to God. Be a thankful person. Thank God
specifically for life and the things and people you enjoy. And
do it many times a day.

I know one dear man of God who makes it a discipline of his
life to say "thank you" to God a hundred times a day. He uses
his fingertips to count off a hundred "thank you's." It may
sound mechanical, but it is his way of disciplining his life in a
way that he considers not only fundamental to enjoying life,
but fundamental also to his spiritual growth.

Let me wrap up this thought with a question: *Have you ever
met a truly thankful person who did not truly enjoy life?*
Enough said.

There Is a Point of Departure

As we near the closing pages of this book, I'm very aware that some of you "out there" may still be unsure of your relationship with God. You may be feeling nothing when it comes to life's meaning for you personally. Possibly, you have never experienced God's love by inviting Jesus Christ into your life. If that be the case, let me tell you here and now that Jesus Christ is ready to offer you His gift of life—abundant life for your present moments, and eternal life to come. And because it is a true gift, it is literally yours for the asking!

You see, the greatest hindrance to enjoying our present moments is restlessness within ourselves. Within the heart of every man and woman there is a void crying out to be filled with a sense of God's forgiveness and His unconditional love, the stuff that provides the foundation for purpose and gives meaning to life. That void is crying out for a right relationship with God, one that each of us was created to enjoy. This "God-shaped vacuum" was placed in the human spirit by God, and can be filled only by the presence of His Son Jesus.

When that void is *not* filled, we can churn with self-condemnation, dissatisfaction with life, and a sense of bitter estrangement from life's meaning. With that void filled by Jesus Christ, there can be a profound sense of peace: peace with God, peace with others, peace with yourself.

Sure, many of the events of your present life—to say nothing of the shrouded events of your future—often seem a mystery. But with Christ in your life, you'll be in a relationship with the One who *as a man* experienced every doubt, burden, and frustration that you feel, but who—as the omnipotent God—can invade your will, your emotions, and your daily circumstances, bringing positive, lasting change.

Let me assure you: now is the time to ask Jesus Christ into your life. Now is the time to let His love and forgiveness fill that aching void. The foundation for a fulfilling present *and* future is bound up in a Savior, and Jesus Christ is that Savior. Again, I encourage you to invite Him into your life as Savior and Lord today. Jesus said, "Behold I stand at the door and knock; if any one hears My voice and opens the door, I will come in to him . . ." (Revelation 3:20 NAS).

In Closing (and in Beginning)

If you've read this far, I believe you'll allow me to say one more thing one more time. BEGIN NOW TO PREPARE FOR YOUR FUTURE. Take what you've learned from this book, add to it, build upon it, and begin planning *now* for your retirement years.

Then to balance your life, begin *living* in the present. And always remember this:

> The future cannot be an end in itself . . . because it can all too easily become an escape from the present. The value of preparing for the future is not only what it can bring to your tomorrows, but also the quality change it can bring to your present life.

I'm excited for you, because you are about to begin your own personal adventure into the best years of your life!

God has prepared the way. He has already given you all you'll need for the future. Your part is to be His partner in prayer and planning, to take possession of what He has provided!

Godspeed on your journey!

> A man's mind plans His way, but the Lord directs his steps and makes them sure.
>
> Proverbs 16:9 AMPLIFIED

What you will be . . . you are now becoming.

Source Notes

1. Reuel L. Howe, *How to Stay Younger While Growing Older* (Waco, Tex.: Word, Inc., 1974), p. 142.
2. Quoted in Chris Barnett, *Flightime*, July 1974.
3. Raymond and Anne Ortlund, *The Best Half of Life* (Glendale, Calif.: Regal Books, 1976), p. 65.
4. David Ray, *The Forty Plus Handbook* (Waco, Tex.: Word, Inc., 1979), p. 12.
5. Anaïs Nin, in *The Crown Treasury of Relevant Quotations*, Ed-

ward F. Murphy, ed. (New York: Crown Publishers, Inc., 1978), p. 491.
6. Jim Conway, *Men in Mid-Life Crisis* (Elgin, Ill.: David C. Cook Publishing Company, 1978), p. 31.
7. Marya Mannes, in *The Crown Treasury of Relevant Quotations*, p. 433.
8. André Gide, in *The Crown Treasury of Relevant Quotations*, p. 433.
9. Conway, op. cit., p. 132.

Appendix
Here's to "Keeping on Course"!

It is my prayer that the facts and principles contained in this book may have charged you with new inspiration and new motivation to begin preparing *now* for your retirement years.

However, experience tells me that motivation can evaporate all too quickly in the atmosphere of life's everyday cares and concerns. I also realize that preparing for retirement is a journey of some length, and—on the way—it is all too easy to forget those important principles that are essential to making the journey a success.

That is why I've prepared the following exercises, which I recommend you review at least once a year. The material is not meant to be a detailed checklist of all points necessary in preparing for retirement. Rather, it includes questions that will jog your memory, and some directives that will help you "correct your course" as you head for your destination.

I suggest you have a paper and pencil handy as you study the material. I'm sure you'll want to write down things that come to your mind—things that you may wish to do, or to follow up on.

As you'll see, the material has been prepared in subject units, each one containing questions to *reflect* on, directives to *act* on, and—finally—closing thoughts to *remember.*

You might want to work on one or two units a day over, say, a two-week period. Or, you might want to go away to the beach or the mountains with your spouse and spend a day with him or her in study, conversation, and meditation.

However you choose to use this chapter, review it at least once a year. I believe it can help "keep you on course" as you plan for the best years of your life—your retirement years!

REFLECT
- When you think about the future and your retirement, how do you feel? Is there a sense of anticipation and expectancy? Or is there uncertainty, anxiety, or worry?

ACT
- Read Matthew 6:19–34 to gain a fresh perspective on your heavenly Father's care and concern for you.
- Thank Him for the provision He has already given you—for the present and for the future.

REMEMBER
- "For God hath not given us the spirit of fear; but of power, and of love, and of a sound mind" (2 Timothy 1:7 KJV).
- "And my God shall supply all your needs according to His riches in glory in Christ Jesus" (Philippians 4:19 NAS).

* * *

REFLECT
- The Bible tells us to trust God and be at peace about our future, but how do you feel about actively planning for the future?

ACT
- Review God's strategy for "partnership" with man. Read Numbers 33:50–56; Deuteronomy 2:16–31; Joshua 1:1–11; and 2 Chronicles 20. Think about how God *gives* and we *possess*—by prayer and faith put into action.

REMEMBER
- "God has provided for our future and it is our birthright to be at peace about it. But it is part of the miracle of being born into the family of God that He has chosen us to be a partner in possessing that which He has provided."
- ". . . [the disciples] went out and preached everywhere, while the Lord worked with them, and confirmed the word . . ." (Mark 16:20 NAS).

* * *

REFLECT
- In the midst of the ever-changing "retirement revolution," have you been careful to keep abreast of retirement's new challenges and opportunities?

ACT

- This month, read through two or three magazines targeted at retirees—publications such as *Modern Maturity* and *50 Plus.* Give yourself an update on retirement trends, new legislation, new opportunities. If you are over 50, subscribe to one of these magazines.
- Review chapters 2 and 3 of this book.

REMEMBER

- "There is no effortless, automatic course toward retirement. Retirement represents one of life's major transitions —a transition that can bring great fulfillment or great tragedy."
- "Where is the man who fears the Lord? God will teach him how to choose the best" (Psalms 25:12 LB).

                                    *   *   *

REFLECT

- Take an emotional inventory of how you feel about your own aging. Are you fighting it? Are you trying to stop the process? Or are you accepting it—even being thankful for it?

ACT

- This month begin a new interest, hobby, or project that places some healthy "demands" on your body, mind, and spirit. You should never stop growing!
- Ask your spouse to stop you every time you "put down" the fact that you are growing older.
- Review chapter 4.

REMEMBER

- "Abundant life is the reward of those who are thankful for life's every season: thankful for the past, thankful for the present, and thankful for the future—including the fact of aging!"
- "I made you and I will care for you. I will carry you along and be your Savior" (Isaiah 46:4 LB).

                                    *   *   *

REFLECT

- Would you say you haven't yet entered any kind of mid-life crisis? Or are you in the middle of "the storm" on the other side?

- At this time in your life, how do you feel about your work? Your marriage? Your family? Your relationship with God? Fulfilled . . . or restless? Are you fairly well at peace with yourself? Your past? Your future?

ACT

- Spend a third of a day reflecting on your feelings about the questions (and answers) above: how you feel about your relationships, your work, yourself. Then, spend the rest of the day in prayer and meditation on the theme of God's unconditional love for you. Remember, God wants your self-concept (your identity) to be firmly locked into His love —not the externals of youth, wealth, success, and so forth. Read *Lord, Make My Life a Miracle*, by Ray Ortlund. Read Scripture portions such as Jeremiah 31:3; John 13:1 and 15:9, 13; Romans 8:35; Galatians 2:20; Ephesians 3:17–19; and Psalms 103:3–5.
- If you are between 35 and 50, reread chapter 3, Navigating the Mid-Life Storm, or buy a Christian book dealing with the transition of mid-life. It will help you identify some of the things you are feeling, and give you a clearer perspective on what is taking place.

REMEMBER

- God wants to liberate us from a self-concept firmly shackled to the externals—things that change and decay—and He wants to bind our identity closer to His unchanging unconditional love.
- "I am loved, I am loved; I can risk loving you; For the One who knows me best loves me most."[1]

* * *

REFLECT

- During this past year, have you been speaking more openly about the reality of physical death? Even the inevitability of *your* death? Has there been less denial, and hence more acceptance of the fact?

ACT

- Make a covenant with yourself this week to converse with two people about the reality of physical death, and the reality of eternal life.

REMEMBER

- "The fear of death causes us to clutch at life. But Jesus has broken the power of fear and would have us open our 'clutching hands,' as it were, and give not only our lives to Him, but also the moment of our death."
- "For whosoever wishes to save his life shall lose it; but whoever loses his life for My sake shall find it" (Matthew 16:25 NAS).

* * *

REFLECT

- Do you know your net financial worth? Are your figures current?
- Do you know if your Social Security benefits are being correctly credited to your account? Do you know the details of your profit-sharing or pension plan (if you have either or both)?
- Have you begun a retirement investment program? What about savings? Life insurance? Buying your own home? Stocks? Real estate?

ACT

- If there are too many negative answers above, *this month* commit some time to reviewing chapter 7, sitting down with your spouse, and planning your financial future. (Note: You may need to call on professional guidance, someone to help you plan a program with both short-range and long-range goals that will help you move financially toward retirement.)

REMEMBER

- "Whatever your age, you need to make sure you are managing your finances and that they are not managing you."
- "Riches can disappear fast . . . so watch your business interests closely. Know the state of your flocks and your herds; then there will be lamb's wool enough for clothing, and goat's milk enough for food for all your household . . ." (Proverbs 27:23–27 LB).

* * *

REFLECT

- Are you investing some time in a sport or hobby that can bring you satisfaction and fulfillment in your later years?

- Are you spending some time *now* developing a hobby—or perhaps an ability connected with your current career, one that can provide meaningful work (and perhaps even income) during your retirement years?

ACT

- This month, commit yourself to broadening your interests in two areas. One: in some area of recreation. Two: in learning or developing some talent, ability, or gift God has given you. This should be something that "stretches you," that contributes something to others, that is personally meaningful to you—and that could perhaps even produce income.

REMEMBER

- "The sad epitaph of too many retired people is that they equated retirement with retreat. Instead of retiring to the involvement, risk, and growth of *something* . . . they retired to the isolation, safety, and decay of *nothing.*"

* * *

REFLECT

- How do you feel physically? Do you have enough energy? How's your weight? Do you get enough exercise?
- How long has it been since you had a thorough physical exam? (Be honest!)
- How would you describe your emotional "outlook on life"?

ACT

- If you haven't had a physical exam this year, make an appointment this week.
- Reread chapter 9 of this book.
- Go to a reputable health-food store and purchase a book on the "why's" and "wherefore's" of eating nutritiously—and begin following the advice.
- If you're overweight, today is the day to cut back on the amount of food you eat—and on all desserts! (This is still the best reducing program ever devised!)
- Commit yourself to some type of physical exercise. Don't go "whole-hog," but do begin a moderate program that you are likely to continue.
- This month, read one inspirational Christian book and one

informative secular book. Keep your mind exercised by stretching it!

REMEMBER
- "Take control of your body. Begin giving it the right 'orders'—and care. Begin to order your life and fill your thoughts with the stuff that will make you the person you want to be."
- ". . . your body is a temple of the Holy Spirit . . ." (1 Corinthians 6:19 NAS).

* * *

REFLECT
- During the past year, have you been building friendships? *Lasting* friendships?
- How many casual friends do you have (that is, people you just casually "know")? How many close friends? How many intimate friendships?
- If you do not have enough (or perhaps *any*) really close friends, what do you believe to be the reason? Fear to take the first step? Fear of rejection? (Perhaps you don't want to invest the time required.)

ACT
- Think about three people with whom you would like to build close friendships.
- Review your acceptability before God, and the fact of His love for you. (Even though friends may reject you, God *never* will.)
- Risk taking positive steps in moving toward those people— getting to know them better. *Do it this month.*

REMEMBER
- Real friendship building takes time.
- "My loving may be rejected or betrayed. I can be hurt and disappointed by the response, but nothing and no one can take away from me the increase I experience because I love. Therefore, when I love, I am investing in the future of my becoming . . . ."[2]

* * *

REFLECT
- Do you enjoy the small moments of the present? The experiences, the people, the little things that make up the

now of your life? *Or are you restless in the present, ever-involved in activity that will bring fulfillment to your life . . . later?*

- Are you satisfied that your present experiences have meaning—both the good experiences and the bad? Are you at peace with the fact that your life has purpose?

ACT

- Decide now that tomorrow you will stop and enjoy three "moments" of life. One in the morning before the activities of the day; one during the workday; and one in the evening. It might be a sunrise, a flower, holding your spouse's hand, reading the paper, conversing with friends, greeting your family. As you experience the moment, reflect on it—then thank God for it. (If you can, express that thanks aloud.)
- Talk to your spouse about the importance of reminding each other to live in the present. Share together today the enjoyment of experiences you have *today.* If either sees the other repeatedly living in the emotion of a future experience, remind him or her of the necessity of living in the present.
- As you pray daily, begin to thank God for His great provision for your life. Thank Him for ordering your steps. Thank Him *in* the midst of every experience, no matter how difficult the experience might be.

REMEMBER

- *"It is only as you learn to enjoy the present moments of life that you will be able to enjoy your future.* The future does not hold within itself any miraculous elixir that will enable you to enjoy it. *That has to be learned in the present."*
- ". . . all things work together and are fitting into a plan for good to those who love God and are called according to His design and purpose" (Romans 8:28 AMPLIFIED).

Source Notes

1. William J. and Gloria Gaither, "I Am Loved," Gaither Music Publishers, 1978.
2. Reuel L. Howe, *How to Stay Younger While Growing Older* (Waco, Tex.: Word, Inc., 1974), p. 47.